Asians ahead after the first round?

European University Studies
Europäische Hochschulschriften
Publications Universitaires Européennes

Series III
History and Allied Studies

Reihe III Série III
Geschichte und ihre Hilfswissenschaften
Histoire, sciences auxiliaires de l'histoire

Vol./Bd. 780

PETER LANG
Frankfurt am Main · Berlin · Bern · New York · Paris · Wien

Georg Bruchhof

Asians ahead after the first round?

Indo-British Economic Relations from 1939 to 1950

Political and economic aspects of the "Transfer of Power" and the change from direct rule to indirect influence through Western financial and economic supremacy

PETER LANG
Europäischer Verlag der Wissenschaften

Die Deutsche Bibliothek - CIP-Einheitsaufnahme

Bruchhof, Georg:

Asians ahead after the first round? : Indo-British economic relations from 1939 to 1950. Political and economic aspects of the „Transfer of Power“ and the change from direct rule to indirect influence through Western financial and economic supremacy / Georg Bruchhof. - Frankfurt am Main ; Berlin ; Bern ; New York ; Paris ; Wien : Lang, 1998
(European university studies : Ser. 3, History and Allied Studies ; Vol. 780)
Dt. Ausg. u.d.T.: Bruchhof, Georg: Britischer Rückzug aus Asien - Etappensieg der Asiaten?
ISBN 3-631-33280-7

ISSN 0531-7320
ISBN 3-631-33280-7
US-ISBN 0-8204-3591-0

To Marion

At the stroke of the midnight hour,
when the world sleeps,
India will awake to life and freedom.
A moment comes, which comes but rarely in history,
when we step out from the old to the new,
when an age ends,
and when the soul of a nation, long suppressed, finds utterance

Jawaharlal Nehru

Preface

In 1997 the last British colonial territory, the Crown Colony of Hong Kong, was returned to China. The new sovereign, the Chinese People's Republic, was given back its territories after the 99-year lease of 1898 had expired. This transfer will influence Chinese-British economic relations at the end of this century and even more so in the twenty-first century, predicted to be the Asian century. During the last few decades, Hong Kong has become a Far East finance and service centre, a competitor for Japan and the Tokyo stock market. Unlike the process of the *Transfer of Power* in 1947, in which governmental powers in India were given over to a nation not yet in existence, the Crown Colony of Hong Kong was, in accordance with the lease of 1898, returned to the People's Republic of China, which has existed since 1949. The original agreement pertained to parts of the colony, but negotiations between the Chinese and the British government in the 1980s prepared the way for its complete return to China. Article Five of the *Basic Law* foresees a special economic status for the former British territory during the first fifty years following its return. Comparable to 'article five' was the interference of the British business lobby in the *Transfer of Power* from the British to Indians in 1947. These business interests were protected in the form of constitutional *Safeguards* at that time. British business demanded that economic privileges for the British in the colony's constitution of 1935 be taken over into the new constitution. This attempt failed, but the British government, with the help of the USA, retained its financial influence in India after independence. Now that Hong Kong has been returned to China, Great Britain will find it harder to safeguard any special rights negotiated for the Hong Kong region in Communist China. The reason for this might probably be found in the prospering economic situation and increasing strength of the Chinese national economy in the 21st century, contrasted to the relatively weak economic situation of Great Britain.
After the Second World War, the British government had to react politically to its weakened economic position in the world and initiate its retreat from South Asia. At that time, the spirits of victory in the Second World War were still high and Britain was still conscious of old Imperial dreams, pushing aside the facts of losing its position as a world power. Tension had been growing for decades, resulting from national conscience and self-glorification as a world power on the one hand, and fundamental financial and economic facts on the other. This tension was felt in certain economic and political circles during the Second World

War, but only after the Second World War was over, did the public become fully aware of Britain's situation.

This book will treat the British retreat from Asia as a fact and view *Asians ahead after the first round?* as a working hypothesis. As to whether the Asians really was are ahead, this we will be better able to judge in the next century. How we judge will depend on whether predictions of a global shift of economic centres should turn out to be true.

Heidelberg, in December 1997 Georg Bruchhof

Content

1 Introduction

Starting in September 1939, India was increasingly forced to accept the transformation of its economy from one for civil use into one for wartime organisation. In the course of the Second World War, the whole of wool production, all of the shoe and leather-clothing production fell under the dictate of an economy oriented to the necessities of war. Also effected were the entire timber production, almost 75% of steal production, more than 75% of cement production and, in addition to 600 million yards of cotton exports, nearly 20% of cotton textile production. The Indian transportation system suffered from the increasing relocation and sending of military forces and their supplies to changing front lines in the east of India. Reductions in coal deliveries caused questionable restrictions in domestic mining. In addition to these restrictions, there were also cuts in the imports of important consumer goods in the wartime years of 1941 to 1944. Supply cuts for the civilian population went hand-in-hand with an increase in the burden of defence and military logistics. The latter heated up inflation and, since prices were climbing, decreased purchasing power for the common people. Europeans in India were not as heavily affected by inflation as the native population.

This is how Sir Hydari reports on the situation of British-India at the time of the Second World War. India had fulfilled its role as supplier of war-necessities and strove - now that the Second World War was over - to carry through with its demands for national independence. During negotiations in 1942 this had already been among the suggestions of the *Cripps-Mission*. Another milestone in the battle for India's independence seemed to be within reach, Britain's retreat from India and the 'retreat' of its influence in the Indian principalities. There seemed to be headway in both areas. There had been the Montagu-Chelmsford reforms of 1919, the Simon reforms, the passing of the Government of India Act of 1919 and of 1935 (these served as models for working out the Indian constitution of 1950 and thus enabled quick acceptance of the *India (Independence) Act* of July 1947); following these reforms, political and economic events were concentrating on the developments in the post-war period. After the end of fighting in Europe, the Indian sub-continent became the strategic centre of interest for the allied powers for the remaining months until final defeat of the Japanese in Southeast Asia. The conclusion of peace in Europe and Asia accelerated the transformation of colonial India into an independent nation. Significant factors in this process were the leading role of the United States in the drawing up a new international economic order, the convening of an international conference in Bretton Woods in 1944, and its repercussions for the economy and the finances of Great Britain.

The amount and kind of development in the Indian economy during the Second World War will be shown in the next chapter. The discussion will focus on economic aspects of Indo-British relations; these were characterised by the wartime economy and various control mechanisms, controls over foreign trade and currency controls necessary in a wartime economy. The Anglo-American loan agreement of 1941 will also be taken into consideration here, as this led to the financial dependency of Great Britain on the US, which then had repercussions for Indo-British economic relations and also for the finance policies of Great Britain and India. Further consequences of the agreement became especially apparent in the post-war era. Great Britain could only prolong its *Pound Sterling* debts within the *Pound Sterling Area* with the help of a moratorium supported by the United States.

2 Indo-British economic relations at the beginning of the Second World War

It is not easy to understand the nature of Indo-British economic relations. Wee they based on inequality, one party taking an advantage, another trying to do so? Did the relations act to balance out the demands of both sides and lead to economic partnership and co-operation?

In the course of the Second World War, economic relations between Great Britain and India changed.

The first eighteen months were marked by a period of relatively normal trade. India's balance of payments in foreign trade was nearly in equilibrium or even to India's advantage. Imports from Great Britain and the United States were offset in value by exports from India consisting of food and raw materials.

The situation changed in December 1941 when the United States and Japan entered the Second World War. India now became a base for supplies and operations in the Far Eastern theatre of war. The markets in Burma, the Far East, and in Japan as well had disappeared, without being replaced by satisfactory alternative markets for Indian goods in the area of the Indian Ocean and the Middle East. The imports of US-American goods stopped abruptly. War-relevant goods were imported on the basis of the *Lend-Lease Agreement*. In the period of 1942 to 1944, the imports of India decreased considerably, and at the same time India achieved a high surplus in its trade balance, imports based on the *Lend-Lease Agreement* not being included in the official trade figures.

None the less, of what nature were Indo-British trade relations at the beginning of the war?

2.1. War-time economy

With the start of the Second World War – Great Britain's declaration of war on Germany on 3 September 1939 – there was a substantial change in trade relations between Great Britain and India.

On 3 September 1939, the government of India enacted several ordinances. His Majesty's General Governor acted on the basis of Article 1, Paragraph 102 of the *Government of India Act, 1935*. This article granted the Viceroy special powers in the case of war or constitutional crisis. In this way, *Ordinance Number Five* allowed the implementation of special measures to ensure public security and of measures for the defence of India. These measures granted special powers in legislative, executive and judiciary areas. This ordinance was entitled *Defence of India Ordinance, 1939*.

It applied to the whole of India and British subjects in all parts of India, including also the Indian principalities. The measures specifically covered legislation ensuring the defence capability of India by land, naval and air forces.

In 35 points, defence capability was governed in chapter two of the *Ordinance*. Among those included were interventions of the government in the economy, with following paragraphs establishing more detailed provisions.

Paragraph 20 and 21 described economic control measures, paragraph 22 laid down measures of currency control.

Section 14 of the *Ordinance* laid down provisions for finances and precautionary measures; these included measures such as:

- -currency trading ban
- restrictions on the purchase of foreign currencies
- control of all currency dealings.

Private currency trading was also controlled by the government of India and the *Reserve Bank of India*. Section 15 of the *Ordinance* governed restricted trade with the enemy.

Section 12 of the *Ordinance* summarised control of the industry. Paragraph 81 governed the total control of the industry, including all companies and business projects. The government of India was empowered to provide defence capability and provide for the military forces and the civilian population. Measures foreseen:

- imposing production or distribution bans
- dictating prices and expropriating manufacturing plants if required by wartime conditions.

Freedom of trade was limited to those areas relating to India's defence ability, war-time production and the guaranteeing of vital goods for the population. Infringements of this government ordinance were punished by imprisonment.

To guarantee that raw materials remain in British hands, the government of India enacted in paragraph 82 of the ordinance a limitation on the transfer of mines.

Concerning the area of currency control, the *Finance Department* in India announced the import ban on *Pound Sterling* banknotes in accordance with Paragraph 19 of the *Sea Customs Act of 1878*. The *Reserve Bank of India* was allowed to make exceptions.

On Monday, 28 July 1941, the Defence Co-Ordination Department of India made further orders giving the government of India more power. In an announcement on 28 July 1941, the limitations and bans laid down in *the Defence of India Act 1939* were extended to countries not under British sovereignty.

At the beginning of the Second World War, the Indian principalities had promised to co-operate and supply material and human resources. Now, in accordance with the constitution, the special full powers of the General Governor and the Indian government were officially extended to the Indian principalities.

In a further announcement on 12 July 1941, the General Governor extended the *Defence of India Rules* with additional clauses, following Paragraph 2 of the *Defence of India Act, 1939*.

Further clauses were added especially to Order 92, which regulated foreign currency trade. *Sterling Area*, *security* and *transfer* were more closely defined, and currency regulations set down under the existing conditions of the war.

The *Sterling Area* was a kind of 'social agreement'. It went back to a hundred-year-old tradition. Export trade in the British colonies was controlled by British merchants in London who had their markets in the colonies. Export trade was calculated on the basis of the *Pound Sterling*. Goods from the colonies were shipped to Great Britain. The London banks set up subsidiaries in the colonies, and these subsidiaries credited the export revenues to the merchants. There were no local financial institutions. Under these circumstances, English banks overseas did not need to worry about foreign currencies. The *Pound Sterling* was accepted as the international means of payment. If trade was conducted with non-sterling countries, the foreign currencies were converted into *Pound Sterling*. In this way, the dominions of Canada and Australia were able to carry on trade with each other without problems. The only prerequisite was that each country had to have enough of the trade partner's currency at its disposal. Differences were paid by the London *clearing* banks. For this reason it was necessary to have a foreign currency pool, the *Empire Dollar-Pool*. The members of the *Sterling Area* paid into this pool. The spending of foreign currencies was closely monitored by London in order to avert wasteful expenditure of foreign currencies. Thus currency control meant preventing *sterling* from accumulating or aligning in uncontrollable individual or collective circumstances. The mandate of currency control was given over to colonial governments, thus granting them freedom of operation in formulating import policy.

In the *Defence of India Rules*, considerable attention is given to *blocked accounts*. This term designates blocked accounts at the *Reserve Bank of India*. In India, these were not accessible for third parties. Only the *Reserve Bank of India* in conjunction with the *Bank of England* and the government of India could dispose of these blocked accounts.

When the British government announced that it was securing the production of wartime materials, this meant that economic relations and industrial centres of production were to be subordinated to wartime goals. This also meant that the Indian government was given the responsibility of using Indian raw materials as effectively as possible. This resulted in a series of tasks and problems.

First, wartime production affected the economic development of India, the estimation of the social status of the Indian population and the possibility of conflict in India.

Second, wartime production affected plans for natural resources and the information necessary for this purpose.

Third, wartime production brought with it an extension of the special powers of the Indian government.

On 17 November 1939, Horace Wilson of the British Treasury wrote to Findlater Stewart at the India Office of the *Overseas Trade Department* that the interdepartmental committee *Economic Policy* had discussed aspects of 'priority policy.' This meant nothing other than that all measures would be taken to secure the reserves of production and finance. That required a central organisation that would undertake the responsibility of collecting necessary data and analysing civilian and governmental demands on reserves in order to secure the programmes of the various departments. Information was thus collected about governmental decisions, among other things about the limiting of consumption, the limiting of imports and the development of substitute goods. Lord Stamp was economic co-ordinator and director of the central information service.

In order to carry out the limits, prescriptions, and controls laid down in the *Ordinance* of 3 September 1939, the government of India set up the so-called **'Economic Resources Board'**. The initial session of the board took place on 9 October 1939 in the official residence of the Indian minister of trade. Chairman of the committee was Sir A. Ramaswamy Mudaliar, the Indian Minister of Trade. Dr. Theodore Gregory, the *economic advisor* of the Indian Government, was selected as vice-president. Other members of the *Economic Resources Board* were:

- Mr H. Dow
- Sir Alan Hoyd
- Mr C.E. Jones
- Mr M.S.A. Hydari, who directed the mission of Indian representatives to London in 1945
- Sir Guthrie Russell
- Dr J. Mathai, co-author of the so-called *Bombay Plans* of 1944
- Mr P.M. Kharegat
- Mr G.S. Bozman

- Lt.-Col. H-P. Radley
- Mr. T.S. Pillay, the secretary.

The *Economic Resources Board* co-operated with the ministries of the Indian government. Its responsibilities were to:

1. Prepare statistical, financial and business information about the economic situation in India, in order to aid the decision-making process of the various *departments* of the Indian government.
2. Maintain contact with the *High Commissioner for India* in London and keep the government informed about the development of commercial and financial legislation in the Empire.
3. Provide the departments of the Indian government with economic memoranda and expertise.
4. Compile a report on the economic actions of India within the framework of its economic efforts.
5. Report on social conditions in India and propose solutions to whichever governmental department is concerned.
6. Provide general economic data to the provincial governments and to the Indian principalities, and advise these on request.
7. Prepare and distribute press information about economic conditions in India.
8. Work out plans for more efficient use of the wartime economy together with departments concerned and with the help of expert committees and to compile a report on the results of these plans.

The *Economic Resources Board* was filled with personnel for the most part by members of the *Statistical Research Branch* and the *Office of the Economic Adviser* of the Indian government.

Beneficiaries of this commission work were the provincial governments of India and the central government in New Delhi. Apart from a few exceptions, the *Economic Resources Board* did not act as an executive organ. Executive powers remained in the hands of the ministries.

One of the principle duties of the committee was to accompany the process of industrial development in India and its planning. Committees were set up ad hoc with industrial representatives and experts to solve problems facing the country.

The *Economic Resources Board* consisted of representatives of the following Indian governmental ministries:

- Supply
- Finance
- Commerce

- Labour
- Education, Health and Lands
- Defence Co-ordination
- Imperial Council of Agricultural Research

As to what extent the existing Statistical Branch of Economic Adviser's Office was integrated into the work of the Economic Resources Board, this remained open. The Department of Commercial Intelligence and Statistics and the Statistical Research Branch continued their work until the end of the fiscal year 1939. After the beginning of 1940, according to Dr. Gregory, the results of the departments mentioned above were no longer published. There was an exchange of information between the offices for statistics and the Economic Resources Board. The area of competency for the Board remained controversial. Whereas Dow wanted the competencies of the Board as broad as possible, the majority of the committee decided to leave work and responsibility to the ministries in the government. Consulting the Board in economic matters was left up to the ministries, as part of their area of competency. Kharegat proposed that all proclamations resulting from the 1939 Ordinance and concerning the general economic life of India should be discussed with the Economic Resources Board. Sir Alan Lloyd replied that this was a question of executive powers, which was, however, exclusively government business. Dr. Gregory defended Lloyds position, and in order to appease his Indian colleagues on the committee, he proposed weekly reports as a compromise. These would be a way of getting the Board to submit possible solutions to the respective ministries.

There were also the questions of organising the *Supply Department* and of promoting industrial planning and co-ordination of Indian industry. These Mr. Dow, representative of the *Departments*, answered with the statement, that everything was being done to promote war-relevant industries. Only the matter of civilian consumption presented a problem.

The parties then agreed that the ministries of the Indian Government would consult with the *Board* in all matters and submit weekly reports to it about orders, proclamations and decisions concerning the economic life of India.

In addition to the *Economic Resources Board*, the government of India established a further control institution, the *Tariff Board.*

TARIFF BOARD

This was established by the government of India at the beginning of 1940 for the purpose of promoting exports in special export areas. Governmental subvention of certain export branches was part of its duties and thus, for a while, the protection of the goods produced.

Its powers included the support of existing or newly developing industrial branches during the war. Further, the stimulation of industrial production centres for the war effort was incumbent on the *Tariff Board*. A further task was to monitor the industries sponsored, making recommendations that would safeguard, secure and shape centres of production, as the government had promised to industry. The *Board* also had the duty to report about changes in wartime production cost factors and about the volume of imports. This duty extended beyond the simple determining of cost to suggesting alternatives to production costs and to eliminating wholesalers and mediators in trade.

Advisory activity for the government also included recommending ways of minimising production costs. This was especially important with respect to imports of raw materials and to payment difficulties that would result after the war from the heavy burden of foreign debt.

Another duty of the *Tariff Board* was to protect the Indian market from foreign dumping products.

In the area of customs and raising of customs, the *Board* had the responsibility to determine what consequences the level of custom duties on certain articles had and what effect lowering custom duties had on certain articles from certain countries.

In a report to the government, the board presented trade restrictions favouring industry: production quotas, higher custom duties and further possible protective measures.

In its first working session on 9 October, the *Tariff Board* presented its working method. With a few exceptions, the *Board* did not have any executive powers to carry out. These were incumbent upon the appropriate ministries of the Indian government. The chairman of the *Tariff Board* had an advisory relationship to the provincial governments of India. Instructions for the provincial governments were, however, sent by way of the appropriate ministries in the central government. In the course of the war a new task presented itself to the *Board*. Committees were set up ad hoc to advise over the industrial development in India as the course of the war made necessary.

2.1.1. Import and Export Control

To safeguard the wartime economy, the Indian government issued a number of directives concerning imports and exports. The Overseas Trade Department of the India Office co-operated with the British Board of Trade and with the British Treasury.

The "power to prohibit or restrict the import and export of goods" was already to be found in the *Ordinance* of 3 September 1939 in Part Twelve, Paragraph 84.

Just before the outbreak of the Second World War, on 26 August 1939, the government of India had published a list of prohibited exports of diverse instruments and chemicals. As with all export prohibitions, it cited *"Section 19 of the Sea Customs Act, 1878 (VIII of 1878)"*. The exporting of articles was prohibited both by land and by sea. Articles affected were closely listed in a supplement to the announcement.

One day after the declaration of war on Germany, the second announcement of import and export prohibitions followed. The only exception allowed to this was a license, that is exemption, granted to the *Reserve Bank of India*.

On 8 September followed the next announcement of an export ban. This time it concerned the exporting diverse articles to enemy territory. Included were hand guns, weapons technology of all types, explosives, all means of communication, tools, instruments, maps and pictures.

An announcement issued the same day prohibited the exporting of raw cotton.

Three days later, the next announcement followed. This time raw materials were covered, such as copper, zinc, nickel; semi-manufactured and manufactured goods; various electrical articles, pumps, metal plates, walnut timber, etc.

During the course of October 1939, amendments were added to the notifications; on 16 October 1939 '*No. 26-W. /5)/39 of the 16th October, 1939*'. The export ban affects the products silk, wool, manila hemp and manila rope.

On 31 October there followed another amendment to an announcement, containing changes in wording to the announcement of 25 September 1939.

On 12 October 1939 the British Treasury ordered the India Office to take all possible measures to preserve currency levels by way of import controls. Since currency control in Great Britain's payment transactions with India were not effective, it was absolutely necessary to limit non-essential import goods, as the other members of the Empire were also doing. Croft of the India Office fought with the government of India for the position of the British Treasury. It was well understood that the Indian government was bound by the instructions of the British government by way of the India Office's Secretary of State for India. The British government secured its influence on the government of India with the creation and filling of a post well-disposed towards Britain, the 'Economic Adviser'. Dr. In a memorandum in November 1940, Theodore Gregory, originally a liberal economist and an advocate of 'laissez-faire' economics, confirmed the proposals made in the Lord Stamp Memorandum of September 1940. Stamp, in his memorandum, demanded a reduction of consumer goods in India and, to achieve this, a limiting of British exports to India. Purpose of this measure was to prevent the flow of *Pound Sterling* into the USA and to increase the *Sterling Area* dollar pool.

Import Controls and Reduced Consumption

With respect to maintaining currency levels, the Indian government had set up a system of import control measures and announced its intention of issuing a list of prohibited import articles. The Indian government copied the British government's practice and took over the method of '*Empire Open General Licence*'. An *Open General Licence* is permission to import listed goods without a special import licence from all or from specially listed countries. The intention behind the measure was to grant licences to Empire countries. An exception was France. There was a delay in setting up the control measures for administrative and organisational reasons that upset the British government. In October 1939 the government of India was ordered to put together a list of import limits on non-essential goods. The expenditure of currency was to be avoided without, as far as possible, hindering the flow of trade.

Indexed goods could be divided into four categories:

1. Unnecessary luxury items that were to be prohibited in any case. Exceptions were imports from Empire countries. Canada, co-operating closely with the USA in currency policy, was not included in the exemption.
2. Goods that other Empire countries could deliver; Canadian goods, and foreign currency goods were not allowed as imports.
3. Necessary goods from foreign currency countries; these could be imported in low quantities, but with strict checking of import quotas.
4. Necessary goods from foreign currency countries with import licence; trade with these countries was not allowed to seriously endanger currency levels.

In April 1940, the government of India informed the British government about measures taken. These measures were discussed with representatives of the Treasury, the Trade Ministry, the Import Licensing Department and the

Department of Overseas Trade. The government of India was the accomplice of British demands. Great Britain's economic situation was a picture of desolation. In order to finance the war, expenditures of currency had to be lowered, export quotas to the USA raised and Indian imports cut, but without destabilising the economies of the individual Empire countries.

The conditions of trade became, however, worse in the next six months, and representatives of the Treasury viewed the Indian government's measures as first 'instalment'.

In order to relieve the customs officials in India, the government in Delhi set up an organisation to issue import licences. A list of import goods from Canada and from foreign currency countries, and an overview of import goods from other Empire counties were issued. This was done to implement the *Open General Licence* without Empire countries discriminating against each other. The import licence list die not contain any good from Canada.

Extent of Restrictions

The restrictions were effective at the beginning of the Second World War for luxury goods and consumer goods at a value of £75 million. Other goods were added, raising the total value of the import licence to £140 million. The list of goods also contained food and raw materials subject to the control systems of the Ministry of Food and the Ministry of Supply. In this case the intention was not to limit imports, but to secure the control of important goods. Most important was, as ever, the special factor of securing currency.

These measures were taken, in order to accumulate US dollars and other hard currencies. They applied only to a selection of imports affecting essential goods from the USA and other hard currency countries, such as Switzerland, the Netherlands, Belgium and Sweden. The measures were extended to imports of normal supplies. Exceptions were war-relevant goods imported by Great Britain. Compliance to these regulations were monitored by the Treasury's *Exchange Requirements Committee*.

From the perspective of the Board of Trade, Great Britain's export policy was to maintain the rate of exports from Great Britain to India as far as British export capacities allowed. Restrictions to deliveries of investment goods were unavoidable. The restrictions also applied to the exports of specific goods made of expensive raw materials.

Once again, what was intended with the import and export controls was to secure the currency and industrial reserves of the Empire. In this way Great

Britain could finance the war with its own means and avoid the trade deficit that experts were predicting would lead the country into problematical debt levels

In November 1939, the Secretary of State for India sent a telegram to the Indian Trade Ministry warning that a refusal on India's part to co-operate with Great Britain in this crises would endanger the war effort. He assured the Indian government in Delhi that control measures such as those in Great Britain would not necessarily have to be taken in India. Nevertheless, despite this statement, the government of India received the order a short time later to introduce control measures comparable to those in Britain. By March 1940 the Indian government was making concessions to the British government in the question of the dollar position.

On 7 December 1940, Croft of the *Overseas Trade Department* of the India Office turned to Sir Arnold Overton of the British Board of Trade. He asked Overton for a statement explaining Britain's export policy in hard currency countries. Representatives of the Indian government were surprised by this policy. They would continue waiting for instructions on how to inform the public in India and for instructions on how to handle imports from Great Britain to India. The British Board of Trade gave its instructions to Sir Thomas Ainscough, the British Government's representative in India.

In his capacity as *H.M. Trade Commissioner in India*, Ainscough wrote on 15 March 1940 to J.J: Wills of the British Board of Trade. He stated that Raisman and J.B. Taylor, Governor of the *Reserve Bank of India*, were afraid Great Britain's export drive would be directed towards the hard currency countries and not towards India.

The *export drive* involved consumer goods and was subject to price control policies.

As the political and economic situation became more critical, a further intervention was necessary in the economy. One might ask why these interventionist control measures were necessary. The restrictions laid down on the Indian government gave fresh impetus to British exports. The measures taken affected primarily consumers, served however to control the entire price system.

Intervention means fixing minimum and maximum prices. In times of war, goods are fixed at a maximum, in order to maintain supplies for the civilian population. These were the theoretical considerations that led to a further memorandum on price control on 9 November 1939. A conference on price control policy met on 18 and 19 October 1939 in New Delhi, and Gregory, the economical adviser of the Indian Government, drew three conclusions:

1. It would be advisable to keep in mind, for reasons of price limits, the necessity of replacement costs as alternative. This would possibly result in a reduction of supplies.

2. The doctrine of *constructive importation* – whether in the narrow or the broad sense – is not a satisfactory guarantee for raising prices in India to a calculated *import parity*.

In general, manufacturers and merchants demand higher prices for goods that can only be manufactured using imports from abroad, especially from hard currency countries. This would be normal in India as well, but price controls were expected to prevent this from happening. Nonetheless, supply contracts and arrangements forced importing from the *Sterling Area*. Indian demand, however, ignored these arrangements, which were to be paid on the basis of global market prices. Global market prices rose, however, as a consequence of the World War, so that Indian industrialists and merchants were asking higher selling prices. Normally these products would be sold at global market prices and would return a profit.

3. With respect to exportable products, preventing a rise in prices was in general not desirable.

Complaints of the Indian Government Against Import Controls

On 4 November 1939 the Indian Ministry of Trade turned to the Secretary of State for India and pointed out that the import restrictions foreseen for India did not appear desirable financially, economically and politically. The government in Delhi would like to see more discrimination in the appraisal of political and economic conditions both in Great Britain and in India. India was dependent on higher customs revenues for balancing its budget deficits.

The *General Licence* method was criticised because the quotas were set using the trade levels of August 1939.

2.1.2. Financial Controls and Currency Controls

On 22 August 1940, the government of India announced currency control measures. In accordance with *Section 19 of the Sea Customs Act, 1878 (VIII of 1878)*, it was prohibited to introduce Pound notes of the Bank of England from abroad, whether by land or by see. Exceptions were granted to the *Reserve Bank of India*.

Assisted by the Secretary of State for India, Leopold Amery, the Indian government enacted on 10 December 1940 *The Indian Finance (No.2) Act, 1940* in accordance with *"clause (b) of sub-section (1) of section 67-B of the Government of India Act, as set out in the Ninth Schedule to the Government of India Act, 1935."*

The bill was intended to limit an increase in war costs and was presented on 5 November 1940 to the *Legislative Assembly* in Delhi for passage. After six days of debate, the *Assembly* defeated the bill, by a vote of 55 to 53. The Congress Party voted against the bill because they were against India's participation in the war. The Secretary of State for India reintroduced the bill, in keeping with *Instruction 36-A* of the *Standing Orders* of the *Legislative Assembly* on 20 November 1940 to the *Assembly*. This time the bill was passed.

On 3 January 1942, the British Treasury published another *Overseas Finance Progress Report*. The increase in *Sterling Balances* prompted the government in Delhi to apply at the Bank of England for a further extension of the Indian Sterling Assets in Great Britain. Criticism was expressed when the Indian government announced the extension of Indian loans for twelve months. The government was afraid that an option to buy would be the equivalent of using this loans in Great Britain and that a resulting increase in prices would provoke criticism in India. It was decided to carry out both actions at the same time.

Thus, on 23 December 1941, an Indian loan at 2.5% and at 3% was announced. The market value was estimated at £8 million and at £58.3 million. In addition, on 5 January 1942, the Indian government announced the repayment of a £69.5 million loan. The Indian *Sterling Reserves* approached almost £200 million in 1942.

The Indian Minister of Finances took a stand on current financial policies in a session of the *Legislative Assembly* on 6 November 1940: the Indian government was supporting the development of Indian industry. With this, the Minister of Finances had especially the production war-goods exports in mind. In addition, industries that were making important war products for India itself. It was incumbent on private investors to promote this branch of industry financially.

The extent of Indian exports in the year 1940/41 was as follows:

Orders received from abroad amounted to 2.25 million yards of jute tent tarpaulin, 3.25 million yards of prime jute and cotton, 12 million yards of khaki material, 14 million yards of tent tarpaulin at a value of Rs. 1.40 Lakhs. fresh

The production of army boots and other leather wear increased to 30 times that of pre-war production levels, and the leather-processing industry was in need of a greater quantity of raw materials.

New chemical production sites were being built to replace European deliveries. 400,000 tons of timber and more than one million railway ties were being made for military purposes. The value of these orders by the British government and the allied armed forces came to Rs. 82 Crores by January 1941.

The amount of Indian assistance to the war effort was becoming unmanageable; a reorganisation of distribution was necessary. The organisation of the *Supply Department* by itself could not cope with the deliveries required. A new way of financing became necessary for Great Britain to achieve smooth production of war materials. Because of this, Britain was becoming more and more dependent on the USA, and Indo-British economic relations were already suffering from this during the war.

2.2. Anglo-American Lend-Lease Act, 1941

The Second World War changed the economic situation of Great Britain. Determined by higher imports, lower exports and exports dependent on the war, the balance of payments and trade balance worsened deteriorate, get worse with countries on a dollar basis.

Imports increased, exports decreased, and exporting in general was dictated by the needs of war; this lead to a deterioration in the balance of payments with countries trading on a dollar basis. The gold and dollar reserves – at the start of the war estimated at £450 million and at expenditures of £150 million per year for the next three years – were not sufficient to cover the extremely swift increase in war expenditures. An export 'drive' to hard currency countries in the spring of 1940 was not able to stop the depletion of reserves. The military defeat on the continent in 1940 and the increased production of war goods necessitated higher returns on exports and made the sale of gold and silver unavoidable. But the hopes of continuing with the arms programme on the basis of balanced payments diminished. The problem of 'dollar imports' was solved by the *Lend-Lease* agreement. Now the problem of acquiring the war materials needed could be approached. As a consequence of its changed economic situation, Great Britain was losing markets to the United States. Great Britain's exports were reaching only a third of pre-war production levels.

In the course of the war, Great Britain accumulated a total debt of £16.9 billion. Imports alone accounted for £12.2 billion. 40%, or £6.9 billion was paid back through Great Britain's services and export goods. The rest of the debt was divided as follows: £1.2 billion in capital sales, £1.2 billion debts to third parties

– debt to India alone was £1.1 billion – and net credits, in particular £5.4 billion from the United States and Canada.

In spite of an increase of $2 billion in currency reserves from September 1939 to December 1940, the remaining gold and dollar reserves were only sufficient to finance the programme for 1941. The approaching crisis was met by the announcement of the *Lend-Lease Agreement* by President Roosevelt of the United States.

'Lend-Lease' indicated the free delivery of goods and services from the United States to Great Britain during the Second World War. The deliveries until 1943/44 were only of marginal significance, but they reduced the problem of diminishing reserves and, at the same time, allowed Great Britain to co-operate with the USA. This reached a peak in *reciprocal aid*, also known as *reverse lend-lease*. $27 billion was granted to Great Britain, and Great Britain granted $6 billion to the US. The *Lend-Lease* programme had serious consequences for Great Britain and forced the country to dispose of its dollar assets and other capital assets in the United States. This took place, in part, with great loss of investments. The new capital assets granted by the US in the agreement served to support the weakened *Pound Sterling* and were seen with suspicion and mistrust. The first payments to Great Britain did not follow, however, until two years after the signing of the agreement. The British government was forced to make use of a $425 million loan from the *Reconstruction Finance Corporation*, an institution close to the US government. Parallel to this, British bonds were issued in the US at a value of $700 million. The US government limited the disposition of *Lend-Lease* payments to expenditures in the interests of American defence. American exporters did not need to fear British competition in the area of raw materials, since the British government had voluntarily agreed to this clause in its *Export White Paper* of 19 September 1941. Similar to this was the well-known Article Seven of the 1942 *Mutual Aid Agreement*, which prohibited Great Britain from discriminating against international trade at the close of hostile activities. It was an attack on the discriminating practice of the British, *imperial preference*. This policy of the British created artificial trade advantages and, in fact, protected British business from unpleasant competition. For this reason, Americans continued the 'attacks' after entering the war on the practice of British imperial preference. Great Britain and the Empire countries gave the United States *reverse lend-lease* without any conditions, giving up scientific advances such as radar, jet and nuclear technology, for free. US pressure kept the British from making deals together with the other allies. *Lend-Lease* was partially responsible for the high level of *Sterling debt* at the end of the war since, in principle, it only postponed payment of debt for the British.

In the further course of the war, US expenditures increased in Great Britain and in other countries of the *Pound Sterling* System, thus elevating British dollar reserves. Roosevelt demanded, without informing the British, that the dollar reserves of the Sterling countries not exceed $1000 million and that excessive debt be reduced to this ceiling. This decision was made at the moment of American withdrawal from allied areas of war. The dollar reserves dropped. *Lend-Lease* payments were made after German defeat only for military efforts against Japan. Keynes wrested a few concessions from the United States at a Washington conference in October 1944, but these were only of short duration. After defeating Nazi Germany and defeating Japan on 15 August 1945, the United States stopped all *Lend-Lease* payments. Great Britain was forced to come up with payments for goods delivered or ordered, such as food and raw materials, totalling $650 million.

The decision was especially hard for Great Britain. Its entire capital was invested in the production of war goods and large segments of civil production had been transformed accordingly. Great Britain was not in a position, financially and economically, to repay its US dollar debts, even if it were to make further cuts in domestic consumption. After the war, Great Britain was forced to approach the United States as petitioner and to ask for a loan. Keynes did this in November 1945. The loan agreed to in December 1945 in Washington was something the British government had been able to prevent during the war, but now, owing to the miserable economic and financial situation, it had no other possible course of action.

Evidence for the government's policy is to be found in *Treasury Overseas Finance Progress Report No. 67*. Here the situation of the British currency, American securities and the *Lend-Lease* agreement is described for the time up to 1942.

On 17 December 1941, the US President had issued an order of intended purpose for the use of the Department of War. He granted the Department of War, within the *Lend-Lease* Agreement, $2.0 billion for acquiring important war materials. This amount had been financed since 11 March 1941 by way of appropriated means. At the same time, the agreement granted a sum limited to $1.3 billion in accordance with *"Section 3(a) (2) of the Lend-Lease Act"*, and an additional sum limited to $800 million for purposes of a not exclusively military nature. The total sum granted to the Department of War was raised from $1.3

billion to $2.8 billion. The funds foreseen were, however, by far not enough to finance the drastic jump in military expenses.

On 2 December 1941 Lord Halifax received a new draft of the *Lend-Lease* agreement. The draft was a concession to the British government concerning the passage *"the terms and conditions thereof shall be such as not to burden commerce between the two countries."* The draft planned further *"the elimination of all forms of discriminatory treatment in international commerce."* The entrance of the United States into the war certainly did not diminish Britain's currency problems. Not the least, the reduction in sheet metal and rubber exports from the *Sterling Area* aggravated these problems by lowering its currency reserves. The currency parity sterling-dollar was seriously endangered for the period of time after the end of the war.

For aeroplane deliveries to the American Department of War, payment of pre-war deliveries to the US were demanded in dollars. This involved a financial scope of $400 million, which would reduce the debt level somewhat.

A memorandum on 10 September 1941 concerning *Lend-Lease* explained export policies more closely. All materials delivered to Great Britain under *Lend-Lease* were meant to support the war effort. This was the guiding principle for all distribution and use of these goods. The British government was to monitor the actual workings of *Lend-Lease* activities and prevent any detouring of *Lend-Lease* goods to private business use.

Lend-Lease goods were not exports. The British government ensured that products for inland consumption reached the same level as would have been attained under *Lend-Lease* conditions.

The British government did not use any goods delivered under *Lend-Lease* as exports to new market areas. Quantities were not allowed to exceed that of American exports. Since Great Britain was mobilising all available means for the war effort, British export trade was limited to the absolute minimum necessary for maintaining the delivery and reception of war goods. At times exports of British goods were limited to satisfying elementary needs of the Empire countries.

The policy of the British government could be summarised as follows:

Materials which were restricted in the United States and which Great Britain received by way of direct payments or *Lend-Lease* could not be exported, unless

- they were used for military purposes, either by Great Britain itself or by the allied armed forces, and it was not available from the United States
- they were exported in small quantities and not cited on distribution lists in the US
- they consisted of spare parts for the British military or British industry.

Export articles could be freely available on the market, as long as these were not designated as *"short supply in USA"*.

Distribution of *Lend-Lease* Goods in Great Britain

The selling of delivered goods for private purposes was prohibited. *Lend-Lease* goods were distributed under the supervision of agencies and institutions close to the government. The distribution of *Lend-Lease* goods was not permitted if it entailed discrimination against American companies. Deliveries of food were a special case. Five to six percent of all food deliveries came from the US. Food deliveries were excluded from the conditions of *Lend-Lease*.

The distribution of food in Great Britain was made by wholesalers, who bought the goods from the British government. The *Ministry of Food* monitored the distribution points and the wholesalers, granting each purchaser the same price. Prices were fixed, exceptions not possible. Thus, Great Britain was able to attain stability in prices. To this end, the British government made £100 million in yearly payments.

Things were quite different in post-war India. The country was ravished by famine, but the Indian government had to pay for deliveries of food in hard currency. India did not receive any low-interest credit form the United States or Great Britain. Furthermore, India was affected by the Anglo-American *Lend-Lease* agreement. The Indian government was obliged to keep its accumulated *Sterling* assets in London tied up as loan capital. Criticism flared up in India when the government in Delhi announced that the 3.5% loans would only be released for repayment twelve months later.

2.3. Export and Import

Which products were allowed as exports to India, which were subject to the prohibition of exports? How did *Lend-Lease* affect London's export and import policies? To what extent did India's government feel obligated to follow directives from London? How much room for manoeuvring, how much freedom of movement, how much competence did the government in Delhi retain?

On 4 March 1941 the British Minister of Trade announced the government's *'production policy'*. Minister Lyttelton placed resources for war production in the middle of the government's plans. Cuts in domestic consumption, the transfer of working forces to wartime industries, and also a reduction in imports were unavoidable.

The British Treasury was especially interested during times of war to keep currency reserves stabile and thus felt it had something important to a say in Indian import policies.

The Treasury wrote to Turner and Baxter of the India Office on 1 February 1941. In the Finance Department at the Indian Office, Henderson was responsible for working out the extent of import and export control measures in India. There was disagreement in the India Office over the Dr. Gregory's views of the 'Stamp Memorandum' of 18 September 1940. Stamp was the *Central Economic Adviser* of the British government, and in his memorandum he demanded, in order to avoid currency expenditures, restrictions on importing and exporting on the one hand, and that a restraint in consumption by the population on the other. Gregory reacted to Stamp's memorandum. He confirmed that expenditures of currency reserves were limited exclusively to imports of war-goods. In order to pay for these, it was necessary to allow exports to the so-called hard currency countries.

On 27 March 1941, the British Treasury wrote to Turner at the India Office. It confirmed sending the Indian import control measures and went on to update the India Office concerning the development of financial and economic policies with Canada. As had the US, Canada granted the British government credit as a consequence of the *Lend-Lease* agreement. The results of the three-party conference in Washington – Philipps, Clark and a representative of the United States – were not affected by this. The British Treasury asked for additional information concerning import restrictions of the Indian government.

There remained the question of who actually was served by the restraint in consumption. Was this restraint supposed to strengthen war-time industries or was it, on the contrary, supposed to secure currency reserves and the overall economy of the mother country? In a telegram from the Secretary of State for India to the Indian Department of the Interior on 30 January 1941, facts were presented that were useful for the talk with Gregory. The telegram was prepared by D. H. Robertson at the British Treasury and signed by Waley Keynes, Kershaw and Baxter at the India Office. India's positive balance of trade was lessening the *Sterling debt* in London instead of importing consumption, which would make prices rise. In this way, India was helping to build up the dollar reserves; Great Britain was trying to evade economic extortion on the part of the United States.

The accumulation of *Sterling* assets of Indian businessmen in London was worrying the British government. It was feared that these might be used in an uncontrolled manner to invest in mutual business interests.

With these changes in circumstances, each ministry no longer made decisions on its own, but the *General Cabinet Committee* and its chairman Sir John Anderson decided measures affecting the economy during the war.

2.3.1. Great Britain

Production in Great Britain shifted more and more from that of an export-oriented economy to a war-oriented economy. Nonetheless, the remaining volume of exports had to be concentrated on hard currency countries in order to build up US dollar reserves. India remained one of the wealth-creating countries for Great Britain, and remained so, under different circumstances, at the end of the war. India was not excepted from the 'export drive' and *"it is desired to satisfy India's requirements to fullest extent possible"*. These 'requirements' would be defined by *"use of Empire's financial and economic resources"*. Great Britain did not export any goods to India that were manufactured on the basis of US dollar raw materials and that might diminish wartime production levels, or that were intended for hard currency countries. The cotton industry in Lancashire was concerned about the increase in exports of Indian textiles to Empire countries, and the India Office was concerned, in the long run, about Lancashire's Empire trade.

Sir Arnold Overton at the British Board of Trade informed the Indian government about the import quotas of British goods by way of the British representative in Delhi, Ainscough.

The British government did everything it could to transform the measures decided on into a stabile political atmosphere.

The export drive and imports from hard currency countries was a finely-tuned policy of the Empire. It meant restriction of consumer goods and restraint for the consumers.

The critical war situation after the defeat on the continent was also a serious blow to Great Britain as one of allied war parties. Two principles guided policy-making after the continental campaign:

1. Raise currency levels and save currency by restricting imports.
2. Maintain a minimum of consumer goods in countries relevant to the support of the war.

2.3.2. India

India's economic situation was integrated into the British financial and economic structure. A number of examples illustrate the difficult situation for India at the beginning of World War Two.

On 17 February 1940, the Secretary of State for India wrote to the Indian government outlining the discussion in London over *"war trade agreement, including a payments agreement"*. With Japan, India's trade balance was positive before the start of hostilities in Europe. For this reason a special trade agreement was foreseen for the time of war. India's export products to the United States and Canada were jute and canvas clothing articles. The British Treasury gave Croft at the India Office an economic prognosis on 14 December 1939. Britain's policy was to prevent importing too much from hard currency countries, as this would raise the danger of growing deficit spending. Free trade was severely restricted in India. Export and import restrictions were worked out by the magical triangle of Treasury, Board of Trade and India Office together with the Bank of England. These restrictions then determined the rate of wartime production. Raisman, the Indian government's Minister of Finance, and J. B. Taylor, Governor of the *Reserve Bank of India*, accepted these controls as necessary measures to protect currency reserves.

The government of India expected an unpleasant reaction on the part of Indian politicians and businessmen. The government decided not to risk a deliberate 'promotional tour' of British goods in India. The awarding of contracts to India's foreign contracting parties was seen as a way to contain profiteering on the part of British business. The classification of imports and the restrictions placed on them illustrate India's import policy.

1. Imports import to industry that could not be procured from other sources
2. Imports from hard currency countries that could be procured from other countries or could even be produced in India itself by developing the necessary industries (import substitution).

Customs regulations in times of war augmented this classification by important war goods and unimportant luxury and consumer goods. In this respect, luxury goods were given taxed with high duties and war-relevant goods with low duties.

India made its tribute to the currency policy of the British government. Trade statistics for the period from September 1939 to January 1940 - in effect the first quarter of wartime economy - used exports to the United States and Canada as a basis for predicting a positive balance in India's trading. India's task was to be the main procurer of currency for Great Britain.

The government of India had to put up with the accusation of its critics that the country was a victim of British economic Imperialism.

The criticism was not unjustified. In a state of emergency and in view of the threat from the outside to national security, the British government took measures that rescinded the concessions made in the *Government of India Act, 1935* and reasserted its economic control function. Great Britain, weakened economically since the Ottawa conference, now took advantage of the wartime situation, seeking to turn the economic order around to the disadvantage of India. In spite of increasing debts to India, Britain's financial and economic position in that country appeared to be untouched.

3 Indo-British Economic Relations during World War Two

Political Background

British export policies had to be adapted to the changes in political and military circumstances. Up until the summer of 1940, the government in London thought that it could manage the fighting against Germany without the financial support of the United States. Export trading was stepped up to this end. In the first months of the war, export production was high, but only very slow progress was made in building up the military. The introduction of production quotas for civil goods was necessary in order to expand the production of important war goods.

In May the German military started a new offensive, putting the British in a dangerous situation. All currency reserves available in Great Britain were invested in aeroplanes, machinery, heavy artillery and other military equipment. It was imperative to acquire currency by way of exports. Since its money supply was only enough for a limited engagement of war, Great Britain felt it could only continue the war effort if it accepted the financial help offered by the United States. The British export economy was practically the opposite of the urgently needed wartime economy. In the initial hot phase of the war, political debates centred on the long-term effects of the war on the currency market and on the loss of important currency reserves.

Another economic aspect of the war must be taken into consideration here. Raw materials were supplied by a number of Empire countries. Import and export measures prevented the uncontrolled flow of raw materials and finished goods important for the war effort. Great Britain had to pay for the delivery of these goods by using credits, loans, or other financial means. The British struggled to maintain the existing levels of trading within the Empire and, at the same time, to enforce strict currency controls. In order to increase its export trade, the British did everything to hinder the development of Indian industry.

Development of Indian Industry during the War

During World War Two, industrial production reached higher levels than in the years before the war. All branches of industry showed increases in turnover. In a short period of time, the cotton industry reached production levels comparable to those of other business areas.

High levels of productivity in main branches of Indian industry such as tea, cotton, jute, leather, coal, iron and steel, were able to satisfying demands before the war. With the start of the war, even small branches of industry were showing productivity growth. One of these was the wool industry, which thrived on orders in the wartime economy. The paper industry was filling production quotas instead of looking for takers and had driven imports of paper off the market. The war helped the chemical industry to expand and produce increasing amounts of sulphuric acid and ammonium sulphate. Wartime orders revived industries in India. At the beginning of the war, the *Department of Supply* was set up in India. This department placed orders amounting to Rs. 56.5 Crores, the equivalent of £42.5 million, including electrical systems and machinery for industrial use, x-ray machines, hospital equipment, footgear, timber, food, batteries, lubrication, acids and other chemicals, textiles, and miscellaneous technological gear.

Not all branches of industry were able to expand during the war. But the potential to do so existed. A few examples will illustrate this.

The cotton industry developed a new product: underwear for the army. Linen was in short supply, and Indian manufacturers came up with a substitute, a combination of cotton and jute.

The quota of imported medical products went from 77% before the war to 46% in 1940.

The Indian government was supporting the development the aeroplane industry in Bangalore. Manufacturing of aeroplane hangers was started in Vizagapatam.

During a budget debate on 28 February 1941, the Indian Minister of Finance stated that contracts amounting to Rs. 1.40 Lakhs had been awarded to Indian manufacturers for 2.25 million yards of jute cloth, 3.25 million yards of jute and cotton balls, and 12 million yards of khaki. Production of army boots, harnesses and leather goods increased to 30 times the pre-war level. Contracts awarded by the British government and the allies amounted to over Rs. 82 Crores. For this reason, the organisation of the *Supply Department* was expanded. The Secretary of State for India promised Indian business the support of the government in Delhi. To secure economic survival after the war, the government laid down plans for protection and generous treatment in tax matters.

On 23 July 1943, the Secretary of State for India L. S. Amery spoke before a meeting of the *Royal Empire Society's 'Institute of Export'* and outlined the necessity for British business to invest in India after the war. As a developing industrial country, India would order capital equipment in Great Britain. This would only succeed on the basis of fair and impartial economic co-operation on the part of both partners. The views of the Secretary of State for India were to remain wishful thinking, as became apparent in the further development of Indo-British economic relations. The political situation in Southeast Asia was precarious, and Japanese occupational forces were on the march. If Indians were to be won over as co-operating economic partners during the war, the Secretary of State for India felt he had to make diplomatic concessions to them in the issue of constitutional reform. Reflections on the Indian constitutional question were tied together with the national economy and India's international position. To what extent was the war a catalyst of industrial development in India? It is a well-known fact that wars change the structure of dependency. During World War Two, from 1942 to the end of the war, India accumulated *Sterling* assets in London amounting to £1.2 billion as a consequence of wartime economy and export directives.

What effects did this accumulation of Sterling have on Indo-British trade during the war? What was trade between the two countries like?

Trade relations between Great Britain and India changed. Trade was supposed to support the fundamental development of industry in India. It was no longer done exclusively on the basis of exchanging Indian raw materials for British finished goods.

The shiploads of British goods to India usually contained war-necessities as well as civilian consumer goods. Machinery, paint, tanning agents and tools made up 45% of British exports to India in the year 1942/43. Of total British imports from India during the same period, 88% were tea, jute, jute products, seeds, pelts, raw cotton, raw wool, tobacco and cotton products.

After the United States entered the war in December 1941, imports from the US to India increased: machines, machinery, tools, tobacco, chemicals, copper, various types of oil, iron and steel, paint and tanning agents, paper and cars. For the year 1942/43, the goods comprised 80% of Indian imports from the United States. The export rate fell at the end of 1943, but in the course of 'lend-lease' deliveries, it re-gained the 1942 level. Imports from the US were offset by a rising volume of exports to the US. India delivered jute and jute products, pelts, rubber-based paint, fruits and vegetables, raw cotton, tea and raw wool. 79% of Indian exports to the US in the year 1942/43 consisted of these products.

India could also show an increase in trade and a equalized trade balance during the war with Australia, Canada and South Africa. The precious metal market also contributed to this equalized trade balance.

Before the Second World War, the price of gold in India was close to the global market price. The price of gold rose after the outbreak of war in the Pacific in 1941; demand became higher and was backed up by stronger purchasing power.

Currency circulation and inflation in India rose due to the increase in demand for war-goods by the western allies, and payments for these goods; economically balanced behaviour of private consumers was far less a factor.

Both Great Britain and the United States had its own agencies for monitoring war-goods. In the US, for example, a '*War Production Board*' was founded.

Great Britain enacted the '*Emergency Price Control Act, 1942*' on 30 January 1942 and the '*General Maximum Price Regulation Order*' at the end of April 1942. Prices for wholesalers were frozen at the March 1942 level.

Scarcity of food and political unrest in 1943 led the Indian government to enact the '*consumer goods scheme*' in 1944. Foreseen was a general loosening of import controls and the importing of various consumer goods from Great Britain. Consumers in Great Britain were angered by this as it meant a reduction in consumer goods offered at home. British imports to India reduced the level of inflation by using up the purchasing power of consumers in India.

In 1945 the Indian government introduced the so-called '*Import Licences*'. Products on the import control list could now be imported. Merchants not included up to then in the privileged circle of importers could finally get into business. The only condition was that the goods had to be imported from Great Britain. In March 1945, the Indian government published the '*Open General Licence*'. The conditions of trade set down therein are summarised below.

The situation for trading was worse in 1942/43 than in 1941/42. Foreign trade had decreased. Exports of private merchants in India decreased in value from Rs. 238 Crores in 1941/42 to Rs. 188 Crores in 1942/43. Imports for the same period fell from Rs. 173 Crores to Rs. 110 Crores. Re-exports of private merchants totalled only Rs. 7 Crores in 1924/43, whereas they had totalled Rs. 15 Crores in 1941/42.

At the same time, war with Japan meant that the allies had lost important sources of raw materials in the Pacific. In January 1942 a '*Machinery of Combined Raw Materials Board*' was established. Its duties were to eliminate purchasing on the basis of free competition and reorganise it on the basis of *Lend-Lease*.

Important Products and Indian Terms of Trade

Raw jute and raw cotton

These were seen as strategic raw materials for the wartime economy. The war meant a loss of 52% in raw jute exports. Up until then, these had gone out to Germany, France, Belgium, Italy and other European nations. *Lend-Lease* deliveries compensated for the amounts lost in exports. From a total of 234,000 tons exported in the fiscal year 1942/43, 89,000 tons were sent to Great Britain and 124,000 tons to the United States. That was somewhat more than half of total exports.

Oil Seeds

The amount produced during the period 1940-43 decreased, in part because of the advance of the Japanese in Southeast Asia and the Japanese occupation.

Peanuts

Production rose in the years from 1940 to 1943. Exports amounted to 258,000 tons in fiscal year 1942/43. In the previous year, 395,000 tons. Principal importers were Great Britain, Australia and South Africa.

Linseed

Exports from India decreased for the year 1942/43 because of lack of shipping space and rising domestic demand. Exports of linseed amounted to only 161,000 tons, after 256,000 tons for the year 1941/42. The British *Ministry of Food* sold the exports at a somewhat higher price from June 1942 on, and was unable to maintain an adequate level of demand. Only 126,000 tons were exported to Great Britain in 1942/43, compared to 212,000 tons in 1941/42.

Rice

There was a crisis in India after supplies from Burma were lost. The war destroyed rice fields and tons of harvested rice. On 23 July 1943, the Indian government announced that it was stopping all rice exports. For the fiscal year 1942/43, rice exports decreased by 48,000 tons, compared to fiscal year 1941/42, and amounted to only 4000 tons more than exports in 1940/41.

In 1943 changes in customs regulations were effected. The *Indian Finance Act, 1943* sent on 29 March 1943 to General Governor Linlithgow was effective for an additional year and regulated duties on salt and cotton. An extension of the 'additional customs duties' until 31 March 1944 was justified by 'section 6' of the *Indian Finance Act, 1942*.

Customs and trade regulations did not suffice to protect British commercial interests in India. Great Britain acquired a considerable portion of its foreign trade proceeds during the Second World War by evading the import and export restrictions of India and by sidestepping Indian competition. The latter was accomplished by way of British export agencies, among others the *United Kingdom Commercial Corporation (UKCC)*. This was typical practice with India and other colonies and dominions.

3.1. UKCC, Trade Promoter in India
Indian Criticism of UKCC Policies

Trade policy. Theoretical outline of export promotions
Practical example: UKCC, British Trade Promoter

Situation in PROMOTING EXPORTS

Since the outbreak of the Second World War, the question subventions for exports had been considered from time to time. The facts led one to conclude that, in an economy oriented mainly towards the production of war materials, exports served primarily to increase the currency supply. Export subventions meant a lower selling price for the goods and thus diminished currency proceeds. This spoke in general against export subventions. Nonetheless, subventions were unavoidable. The cost of production was rising during the war. The exchange rate for the *Pound Sterling* had fallen before the war. Imports were becoming more expensive.

The different positions on the promoting of exports were examined in a session of the *Export Committee* on 31 January 1940. The further promoting of exports was considered in the light of additional losses in the value of the *Pound Sterling.*

The development of matters, despite rising production costs, did not allow the expanding of export subventions. Different markets made necessary different ways of handling export promotions. Exports to the US were subventioned at dumping prices. Many Empire countries granted Great Britain customs preferences. Import controls in many countries of the Empire had the same effect. The aim of export policy was to eliminate the competition of foreign goods.

Many of the markets for British goods were in countries exporting primarily agrarian products. The exchange of currency with these countries was limited by nature. A balance was achieved only by way of an agreement on the basis of deriving mutual advantages, know as *conditional most favoured-status*. Trading was confined to a set quota and a fixed selling price.

Traditional British trading was adapted to the conditions of simple exchange deals. In times of war, however, this type of trading was advantageous for Great Britain.

The instrument of export promotion was the *export drive*. By this numerous possible activities were concealed. One of these was to integrate the various branches of industry into 'export groups'. Another was to set up a national trade association with offices in important countries all over the world. The latter was the *United Kingdom Commercial Corporation* (UKCC).

Below, the *United Kingdom Commercial Corporation* is treated as an instrument of the British government – using legislation during the war declaring a state of emergency – to cement financial advantages over India and to reduce the level of debt to India.

Trade Promotor UKCC

The *United Kingdom Commercial Corporation* was established on 1 April 1940 as a private limited company. Its foundation was the *United Companies Act, 1929*. The British Treasury deposited £500,000 as corporate capital. The missions of the corporation were set down in the *Memorandum of Association*. The UKCC operated all over the world and in every kind of trade. The corporation worked as an independent organisation with permanent consultation of the British government in London. The expressed aim of the corporation was to extend the channels of existing trade relations and not to replace them. The branch office in India was also subject to the rule of involving local merchants in the activities of trade, even in the case of direct UKCC trade with manufacturers.

This statement is important, since this was the 'theory' to be practised. De facto, export figures spoke a different language.

A subsidiary of the UKCC was set up in India in 1941. It operated as a procurement agency and shipping company in the Middle East region. The war limited the merchant fleet and necessitated making deliveries as economically as possible between countries in the Middle East. It was absolutely essential to set up a central purchasing agency with a vast organisational structure, rather than use the normal avenues of trade.

In its first year of existence, the corporation traded in food. The trade in food was stopped at the end of 1942. In its place, goods vital for the war effort were delivered to the Soviet Union up until the summer of 1945. Without a doubt, here the trade corporation UKCC fulfilled useful functions. Deliveries to the extent of the so-called 'Russian Supplies' would not have been possible on the level of private trading.

On 20 February 1942, Rumbold of the India Office wrote to Jago, the President of the UKCC, giving the latter 'free hand' in India. Not only could the corporation make use of the *Supply Department Machinery*, but it could also import and export goods on the import control list, such as steel, textiles, food, jute products and leather goods. The UKCC was billed for use of the Supply Department's distribution channels.

Indian Criticism of UKCC Policies

The UKCC was extremely unpopular in India. Business circles in India suspected the trading company was blocking contact between Indian merchants and their foreign partners and unduly profiting from its capacity as procurement agency and shipping company. Critics accused the corporation of having monopolised the entire export business. The corporation rejected this accusation and pointed out that their cautious co-operation with local exporters was preventing conflict. Nevertheless, criticism of the UKCC remained severe and spoiled the mood of the Indian government. In order to weaken the rising criticism, the government asked the India Office in London for permission to publish notice that the corporation was to be closed at the end of the war.

To meet criticism in the Indian parliament, Nind at the British Treasury gave Rumbold at the India Office justification for the existence of the UKCC in India. The main argument was that the UKCC worked efficiently and brought a considerable volume of trade to India that would not be possible using the usual trading mechanisms.

Miles, the UKCC representative in India residing in Calcutta, travelled to London in January 1942 for a talk with the directors of the UKCC in order *"to be able to give the Government of India some material with which to meet their critics and to calm their fears somewhat as to the future."* Object of Indian criticism was UKCC policy itself and not so much the actual carrying out of this policy. Miles met with the Indian Minister and representatives of the *Commerce Department*. He had an open ear for their wishes. Miles worked in behalf of the British government and was responsible for wartime deliveries to the Soviet Union. His responsibilities also included the organisation of deliveries for military sector of the *Middle East*.

In addition to his capacity as representative of the UKCC, Miles was responsible for providing military projects on India's eastern border with work forces. This was important to the Indian government.

After the debate in the Indian parliament, the competencies of the UKCC were more carefully defined. Employees of the *Supply Department* in the Indian government were given instructions to regulate co-operation with the UKCC. The UKCC was allowed to purchase anything on the free market in India. In delivering important war-goods it could even make use of the *Supply Department Machinery* for those goods subject to export controls.

Methods of payment were clarified after the co-operation had begun. Miles suggested two ways of paying for UKCC deliveries contracted by the *India Office Supply Department*.

1. Settlement of costs by the India Office to the UKCC in London.
2. The UKCC would bill the Indian government for export costs, transfer of payment from London would be to Miles, the local representative of the UKCC in India.

Compensation payments by way of the *Inward London Account Current* were avoided. The India Office in London could no longer check the expansion of UKCC activities in India. Payments were made directly by the Indian government. Numerous deals with private persons were also made, which amounted to the building up of Miles' own organisation.

In the course of the first half of 1942 difficulties arose. Payment transactions of individual UKCC branches ended in chaos. As of 1 July 1942, central directives laid down that separate current accounts were to be set up for making direct payments to the 'head office' in London of *Lend-Lease* deliveries. Payments were in *Pound Sterling* and the difference to local currency was born by the local branches of the UKCC.

A newspaper report delivered an example of the UKCC's economic power. In an article of the 7 June 1945 issue of *Capital*, Sir Francis Joseph, the chairman of the UKCC in London, disclosed the export achievements of the UKCC in India. The trading volume of the UKCC within one month were in the range of 2000 tons of rope, 4.5 million yards canvas clothing, 5200 tons of tea, 2000 tons of peanuts, 24,000 tons of sacking, 909,000 yards of pull-over cloaks made of jute, 1.1 million bags of sugar, 300 tons of shellac and 2500 types of running cotton materials. By way of the trading activities of the UKCC, India helped build up new industries in northern Persia and provide the Soviet Russia with footwear. On the basis of the provisions made by the UKCC to the Soviet Union, Sir Joseph predicted close economic co-operation between India and the Soviet Union after the war.

At the end of the war there was the question of the UKCC's future. Rumbold wrote to Henderson on 27 April 1946, stating that *"there is thus no future in India for the corporation or any similar U.K. organisation."* The British government was rethinking its export policies after the war and wanted to make use of the India Office's experience with the UKCC. The UKCC could operate in underdeveloped countries such as Afghanistan, Persia and Turkey, where doing business was very risky. Trading with countries such as these was politically desirable after the war, but British industrialists were not such trade into consideration in their foreign investment plans.

Rumbold did not advocate replacing private trade with state-operated trading companies. He saw many possibilities for state-operated trading companies to help the private sector in making trade agreements. For this reason he spoke out for retaining the UKCC.

In a memorandum of 23 April 1947 the *Committee on External Economic Policy and Overseas Trade* reached the conclusion that *"a complete state monopoly of foreign trade is incompatible with the type of mixed (private and public enterprise) economy which we are at present creating."* Founding a state-owned trading company would have had an unfavourable effect on export quotas. Exports in 1946, however, needed to be increased. Great Britain's negative balance of trade with the United States made this imperative.

The UKCC in 1946

At the beginning of 1946, with few exceptions, all branches of the UKCC had stopped operations and closed its agencies, as the British Treasurer and the Secretary of State for Trade had decided in November 1945. Only in those special cases where the supply situation was still critical, did the *Ministry of Food* take upon itself the task of buying, storing and distributing food. Branches closed down were transformed into *British Government Purchasing Missions*.

There were doubts about the intentions of closing down the UKCC. The Indian Minister of Trade had to justify the activities of the UKCC during the war before the *Council of States*. The UKCC prepared the minister's statement with the consent of the British Treasury. Thus, it was not possible for the UKCC in times of war to sort out money-losing items. The British government paid for over 90% of handling charges in India and allocated this to the UKCC. This procedure had no influence on the shaping of prices in India, it was maintained. Over 65% of Indian turnover, including ministerial purchases, were civilian goods for the Soviet Union, charged according to the agreement of August 1941 between Great Britain and the Soviet Union. Costs of delivery in addition to this were born by the UKCC and debited to the British government. The rest of the UKCC's deliveries in India went primarily as essential goods to the provinces for building up military facilities and for providing for those already existing.

UKCC Activities as Seen by the Press

The following commentary was published in an article of the 5 July 1945 issue of *Capital* concerning UKCC activities in India:

The UKCC increased its activities in India during the last months of 1945. The UKCC was set up by the British government to provide the allies with important raw materials and other supplies for the war effort. The UKCC became the target of Indian criticism. Indian business circles saw it as a conspiracy of the British government to strangle Indian trade and simultaneously to keep profits in the hands of the organisation. All trading with the Middle East went by way of the UKCC. Items traded were clothing, thread, jute products, consumer goods. A large amount of goods sent to the Soviet Union were bought up by Indian agents. The Indian government denied rumours that the UKCC was to be replaced by a non-Indian company. At the end of June 1941 there was a meeting between the UKCC and representatives of the *Federation of Indian Chambers of Commerce and Industry*. Announcing the closing of the UKCC in India was not enough to silence criticism of the organisation. The Indian government was accused of having granted the UKCC a quasi-monopolistic position in India. Its closing was intended as a way of producing better understandings in trade relations between Great Britain and India.

The Significance of the UKCC for British Foreign Trade

As long as deliveries of civilian goods continued to the Soviets, the UKCC in London would have to make payments for Indian goods delivered; both the British and the Indian governments were bound by the agreement of August 1941.

Maintaining the Indian branch of the UKCC despite vehement political pressure in Indian was politically inopportune. During the final phase of the war, however, the British Treasury insisted on keeping the UKCC in India, even after the war was over. In September 1944 the Indian Minister of Finance discussed criticism of the UKCC with representatives of India business.

Sir Purshotamdas ensured the Indian industrialists that the Trade Ministry of the Indian government would not infringe on the position of Indian merchants.

What was the criticism about and how high were the losses of Indian merchants?

Indian relief deliveries to the Soviet Union from 1941 to 1944 amounted to £8,750,000. The Indian government offended Indian tea exporters by granting tea-export licences exclusively to the UKCC.

The UKCC was of greatest importance for the British export business. The *Board of Trade* issued a memorandum equating the work of the UKCC with Great Britain's economic influence abroad. For this reason, the political agitation of the UKCC in India was of highest importance. In disputes between UKCC and Indian industrialists, the government in Delhi sided with the UKCC and subordinated itself to the wishes of the British government in London. The existence of the UKCC as competitor to Indian merchants lessened the accumulation of Indian *Sterling Balances* in London and eased the terms of payment for the British in India.

3.2. *Sterling Balances* and British Terms of Payment

On 30 January 1941, the Secretary of State for India wrote a letter to the *Home Department* of the Indian government.

"The counterpart of the Indian economy's increased holding of sterling is an increase in the capital assets of individual Indians in India. Up to the present this increase of individual wealth has largely taken the form of increased holdings of coins and notes. In an economy like that of India this is, to a certain extent, natural; and so long as the coins and notes are firmly held by their owners, and expended by them on one another's products, no particular harm is done."

While considering Indo-British economic relations in the period of the Second World War, it is worth while to turn to the development of the *Sterling Balances* and in this context to the British terms of payment.

STERLING BALANCES

In 1943 the *war cabinet* set up a permanent *Committee on Indian Financial Questions* presided by the Treasurer. The committee's responsibility was to initiate anti-inflationary measures, namely to transform a portion of the production of war goods into consumer goods. A further responsibility was to stem Great Britain's mounting debt to India.

In 1943 it was not possible to foresee or estimate the extent of British *sterling debt* to India. There was thought of striving for a 'settlement' with India. The British Treasurer determined that a large part of the sterling holdings came from India's export surplus with other countries of the *Sterling Area* or from Canada and the United States. These trading transactions were closed on the basis of the sterling or the dollar, and credited to Great Britain. London held larger deposits of currency. These reserves were of no direct benefit to the British government, but they strengthened Great Britain's weak debtor position during the phase of negotiating repayments after the end of the war. The Treasurer confirmed that his government intended to direct the negotiations with India in such a way that unreasonable debts and burdens would not befall the British side. The *Defence*

Expenditures were changed. As in the past – in 1940 before Japan entered the war, and also in September 1942 – the war cabinet came to the conclusion that India should share more of the burden of war. The Viceroy in India saw political dangers and discords brewing in the economic circles of India should the proposals of the war cabinet be put into action. Churchill preferred offsetting the British *sterling debt* with a counterclaim and expected the support of his colleagues in this matter. But Churchill realised that his position would find no sympathy with the public or in the British Parliament.

How could British war expenses in India be reduced in order to diminish the *sterling debt*?

British Expense Control Mechanisms

The British government paid for its financial expenses in India at two Indian governmental ministries: the *Supply Department* and the *War Department*. Another ministry, founded in 1943, the *Food Department*, took over responsibilities of the *Supply Department* in providing the Indian population with food.

The *Industries and Civil Supplies Department* took over responsibilities of supplying the cotton industry in India from the *Supply Department*.

Financial control over expenditures of the *Supply Department* and the *War Department* were taken over by the *Finance Department* of the government in Delhi. This was overseen by the *Additional Secretary* in his capacity as *Financial Adviser* of the *Military and Supply Finance*. Financial control over expenditures of the *Food Department* and the *Industries and Civil Supplies Department* was taken over by another department in the Ministry of Finance.

The *Supply Department* had two branches, the *Munitions Production Branch* and the *Supply Branch*, each with its own general director. The first branch was concerned with weapons, production of munitions, tanks, naval matters, railway equipment. The second with wool textiles, clothing, oil products, cars, timber and other necessities for daily life. The entire strength of the *Military and Supply Finance Department* was 72 employees.

Another 128 persons were employed at procurement and control in the *Food and Textiles* section of the *Food and Industries and Civil Supplies Departments*. The *Supply Department* was split up into Head Office, Planning Office and Purchasing Office. Trade deals made were the results of quick consultations in the *Supply Department* and the *Finance Department*. The *War Department* was placed under the supervision of a *Deputy Financial Adviser* who instructed his employees in financial matters. The British Treasury and the *War Department* co-operated closely. Enquiries to the *Supply Department* came directly from the armed forces, the *Central Provision Office* and also directly from the British government. A small number of enquiries came from other ministries of the Indian government. The *Supply Department* did its best to process orders quickly and efficiently. Industrial production centres were also expanded when necessary. In order to finance the needs of war, special cost-cutting measures were required. Controlling unit price costs was particularly difficult in India. A declining number of business partners and rising prices at the same time made reliable calculations of costs impossible. This was one of the difficulties in contracts with fixed prices, and this led to products being set at higher prices for the Indian government. The Indian government could only compensate for the ensuing higher product costs by accepting rising inflation and freeing the prices for everyday consumer goods. The burden on Indians was higher prices and a higher inflation rate, and this hit the poorer classes of the people especially hard.

An example for the differences in profit basis: Indian industrialists made a profit of 7.5% on business with the government and a 50% profit on non-government business. In this manner they made total profits beyond description. Consumers directed their criticism against the government in Delhi. They expected the government to grant business partners higher profits in order to lower the prices of consumer goods. Prices controls and monitoring procedures introduced by the government could not always be strictly maintained because of the small number of governmental and administrative employees.

The problem of the *Sterling Balances* was different, becoming more critical towards the end of the war. Great Britain's *sterling debt* in India alone reached £727 million at the end of December 1943. Of this, £33 million was in the holdings of the *Reserve Bank of India* on 25 August 1939. If repatriation operations had not taken off £310 million of the debt burden by the end of 1943, the British government's debt would have exceeded the level of £1037 million, which is also what happened at the end of the war. More exact estimates as to the rising level of *sterling debt* were not possible during a time of war, since neither the length nor the intensity of the war could be foreseen.

The Indian government was not in a position to carry out further repatriation of the *sterling debt* and considered withdrawing further amounts from the *Reserve Bank of India*, where the money was gathering one percent interest. Instead, the government preferred buying bonds with yields of 2 to 3%. Justification given for this was that British expenses in India were anti-inflationary measures.

The committee *Indian Financial Questions* sought the final solution by working out a financial contract with India at the end of the war. Debts were to be paid off in proportion to economic conditions.

It was obvious why the Indian negotiators agreed to a *Financial Agreement* in 1947, as can be seen from the report given at the end. India and Britain's other creditor nations were highly interested in seeing to it that the value of their assets in Great Britain remained stable. Bonds and the interest on these were part of the financial plans for the post-war era and for rebuilding indigenous industries.

The British Minister of Trade, in a memorandum of 5 November 1934, complained not only about Great Britain's mounting *sterling debts* in India and in other creditor nations and the effect of these after the war, but deduced from all this the danger of a worse economic future for Great Britain. For this reason, the Minister of Finance was in favour of an early revision of British financial obligations. But the war demanded the further production of war goods.

3.3. Production of War Goods

In Great Britain, in the Empire countries and in India, great efforts were made to increase and, if necessary, reorganise wartime production. To this end it was often necessary to lay down a new financial and legal framework. In this respect, the *Supply Department* issued a memorandum. Three measures to increase production were planned:

1. Integrate new industrial systems with existing production centres under supervision of the central government in Delhi.
2. Build new industrial systems in the form of *Managing Agencies* under supervision of private business persons.
3. Combine and co-ordinate existing industrial systems.

The artillery production sites in Lakhnau, Ambernath and Khamaria, gun production in Ishapore, and weapons production in Cossipore fell under the first measure. This accounted for 85% of industrial goods exported to India since the beginning of the war for increasing levels of armaments in the Far East.

The financial scope of the second measure was Rs. 1 Crore. A cable factory was built with the help of the Indian government and managed by a private company commissioned by the government. A private company could serve as a second example; this company serviced aeroplane factories and repaired aeroplanes at four locations. The company worked on commission of the government and was the first to receive right of first refusal on one of the four factories.

The co-ordination of diverse companies by the government, listed above as third measure, cost Rs. 1.25 Crores. A factory with machinery was either loaned or placed at disposal without interest to a private contractor by the government. The government was promised a certain percentage of the proceeds on goods for its part of the co-operation. The government was normally the owner, but a private party could register for right of first refusal.

What were the *supply contracts* like before the war?

These were *open tenders* before the war, that is, they were announced publicly in daily newspapers and in trade journals. The Ministry of Defence ordered few deliveries in the first days of the war, and price was regulated by supply and demand. Up until the end of 1941, trading in cotton textiles could be done on the free market. As more and more capacities were converted to wartime economy, the normal trading and price mechanisms became ineffective. The *Supply Department* handled reception of orders according to *registers of contracting by categories*. Small companies and merchants received preferential treatment and had the liberty of free pricing on products such as knives, forks, household objects, tables and chairs.

Export and import regulations were applied to 'organised industry' to hold down the costs of war and to keep inflation from heating up. For a number of important war goods, the Indian government decided on setting fixed prices plus a profit margin, the *cost plus* system. Here are a few examples:

Automobile Production. Two companies would compete by offering vehicles at actual cost and a set profit margin per vehicle.

Truck Production. 16 larger and 11 smaller contracted companies would compete on the market. One of the larger ones was responsible for half of production. Basis of payment were the fixed costs per unit. The other contracted companies produced on the basis of variable prices.

Production of Army Boots. The agreement was to adjust the price of manufacturing every three months. The price was set by the *Government Cost Account Officer*. The momentary unit price was calculated using fixed price plus a fixed profit of 8 annas 10 pies per unit.

Production of Tyres. The tyre industry was promoted by the government. Unit cost was set at fixed price plus 10% profit.

Although the costs of assembling cars, building trucks and making boots were market-oriented, prices for raw materials increased, and this led the government to dictating fixed prices for production. The companies contracted were large, efficient and well-organised. Prices set by the government allowed for the effect of changes in exchange rates on raw materials.

Steel. Just after the outbreak of war, a contract was settled with the main producers that was to be adjusted to rising import prices. It was agreed that every six months new production prices would be set based on the prices of 1 October 1939. The industry produced Rs. 29 Crores worth of steel yearly, 85% of which was bought up by the Indian government. Production of steel for goods not relevant to the war was offered to the private economy at the usual market price.

Cotton Textiles. Up until the end of 1941 the government in Delhi acquired cotton textiles needed using a competitive tender system. As of 1942, the government closed a contract with representatives of the cotton textile industry in India setting fixed prices, adjusted quarterly. As in the case of steel prices, the highest paid price in June 1941 became the basis for the lowest fixed price. Increases were determined by changes in manufacturing costs that depended on increases in raw material prices.

Cement. The production price of cement was fixed from November 1942 to October 1943. The raw material price rose at the end of the contractual period, and the government contractors, two large cement producers, made losses. For the period from 1943 to 1944, a fixed price was agreed to, but with the stipulation, that flexible adjustments could be made depending on rising costs of labour or materials.

Petrol. This was sold to the armed forces at a fixed price. The armed forces received a discount on the amount they bought. The market price was reset each half year, and the price was set down in an agreement between merchants and the *Industries and Civil Supplies Department*. The agreement was renewed in 1940 and in 1942.

Jute Products. The Indian government signed individual contracts with merchants through the *Adviser on Jute Supplies*, who was also the chairman of the *Indian Jute Mills Association* at the same time. The price was determined by the market price of raw jute at the time of ordering, the average price of manufacturing, a profit margin of 7.5%, and 2.5% *managing agency allowance*.

Timber. This was sold by the *Agency of Provincial and Indian States Forest Departments*. The *Supply Department* set up a plan for each region in conjunction with the *agencies*. These carrying out business by order of the government. Costs were calculated on the basis of pre-war prices adjusted to the estimated rise in costs. Trading was controlled by the government.

Production goods listed above made up 50% of *Supply Department* purchases. It is important to know the extent of obligations in the contracts at the time. The armed forces provided the *Supply Department* with a schedule for making plans. On the basis of this schedule, the *Supply Department* set up the necessary production capacities.

The general policy of the Indian government was a stop on spending for expenses of war, the effects of which became noticed after June 1944. Every six months, every three months from 1944 on, the *Defence Services* corrected their grants of contracts, raising or lowering these according to the circumstances. Contracts over six months were designed so that they could be renewed at any time. All contracts with a running time of more than six months and valued at more than Rs. 25,000 could be cancelled after six months. An escape clause in the contract guaranteed this. This was advantageous to the government, but not the industry. It was advantageous to prevent unnecessary expenditures. Local industries, however, were often confronted with structural problems. Once an industry had adapted to the production of war goods and set all possible capacities in that direction, then a reduction in orders or even a stop of orders would cause very costly restructuring.

All important contracts concerning the above-mentioned war goods included an escape clause. This was not the case for cement production and the automobile industry. The guarantee given was not for the quantity, but for the prices agreed upon. The government had no obligation as to the amount, and therefore an escape clause was not necessary.

But the price policies of the government in Delhi caused trouble. Difficulties in applying fixed prices affected the nature of trading agreements, and putting these fixed prices into effect during the times of unrest from 1942 to 1944 resulted in increased inflation and higher costs for the government.

The Indian government had to pay for its policy of wartime industry price control with political instability; the consumer was at the mercy of merchants and their pricing strategies on the free market.

The Indian masses were not interested in the course of the war and only associated economic difficulties with it. Neither the political nor the economic elite of India saw this war as 'India's National War', and this unrest in the population and in the political class culminated in the uprising of 1942. The general displeasure was fomented by a statement of the *Chancellor of the Exchequer* demanding the payment of more tribute from India. To secure these payments of tribute, the government in Delhi set up a *National Saving Commissioner Defence Board.*

Great Britain had the financial and economic upper hand in India until the turning point of the war in the Soviet Union, despite political unrest and Britain's increasing debt to India. This was not least because of the massive deliveries of war goods to the Soviets, much of which came from India. India's position as Britain's sterling creditor gained in importance almost at the same time as the military turning point in Eastern Europe.

This concludes the summary of the factual side of Indo-British economic relations. The following section shows certain aspects of the forces that determined these relations. Great Britain began to have more and more difficulties in maintaining its financial and economic position in India due to the mounting Indian sterling accumulation.

4 Indo-British Economic Relations before the End of the Second World War

The final phase of the Second World War in India was characterised by bottlenecks in supplies, economic and currency controls, financial and fiscal controls, economic plans for the post-war future, the imminent burden of repaying the *Pound Sterling debts*, and last but not least the political challenge of the *transfer of power* and related constitutional questions. The previous chapter showed India's momentous and important position in the production of war goods. Related to this was India's function as currency procurer of dollars and other currencies for the British Empire's *Dollarpool*. The *Empire Dollarpool* had effects on the tactics used by the British in negotiating the *Sterling Balances* and on Indo-British relations after the war.

Indo-British economic relations were, as already pointed out, still dictated by the British, although Great Britain was becoming more and more India's debtor. Statistics showed India's powerful position very clearly. The surplus of Indian exports to Great Britain surpasses British exports to India by 33%. The extremes of export policies had drastic consequences for India's domestic affairs.

Rising prices, bottlenecks in consumer goods and political riots were the results. The Indian government reacted with price controls. Further control measures were the allotment of raw materials, business controls, limitations for domestic consumers, controls on middlemen and rationing. A governmental decree was issued to secure supplies and the internal distribution of goods for daily life. The government regulated export trading of individual companies. A list was drawn up of the most important industrial contractors. These were expected to resume production of exports after the end of the war. Regulations hindering exports, such as *Export Licensing* and *Statutory List* were to be repealed at the end of the war.

The goal of export policy in Great Britain for the period at and after the end of World War Two was to achieve a surplus in exports in order to meet international payment demands after the war.

For this reason, efforts were made at that time in India to keep the centrifugal effects of the individual state governments in questions of India's economic development under control. Some of these governments strove for an economic development that would be independent of Delhi. A memorandum of the Indian central government on 2 March 1943 outlines a model of central supremacy and veto power designed to reign in separatist tendencies of the state governments.

Was this the beginning of teamwork between the colonial power Great Britain and the Indian independence movement, the *Indian National Movement*? A teamwork in the form of economic development plans worked out by Gregory, the *Economic Adviser*, on the one hand, and in the form and person of Nehru, on the other, who did not tire of demanding political unity for the sake of economic unity?

A unified national territory with a unified economic area would make it possible to exhaust the economic potential of the country. From a financial and political point of view, it is easier and better to negotiate with but one central power in economic and monetary matters than with several competing, sovereign economic units.

Solving these questions would concern India during the following years: How would India develop economically? What form would economic relations between India and Great Britain take on? Between the Indian principalities and Great Britain ? How could the constitutional question raised in India be clarified? How much independence could the Indian principalities afford in questions of economic co-operation after the end of the war. Up to that time they had stood in the shadow and protection of Britain's colonial power.

The British government often spread propaganda about the necessity of co-operation between India and Britain. There were differences of opinion between the British government and British business as to the approaching visit of an Indian commercial delegation in Great Britain.

What did the British government and British business expect from the approaching consultations with leading Indian industrialists in Great Britain? Was there not the danger of British economic interests being played off against American interests when the Indian delegation travelled to North America to sound out the United States?

4.1. Indian Business Delegations in Great Britain and in the United States

What was it, concretely, that made the British and the Indians co-operate economically together? Economically, the British see themselves faced with the challenge of raising their exports in order to pay back their debts to the United States. Indians were giving up involuntarily consumer goods and accepting import and export controls, price controls, currency controls and inflation. Many of the major Indian industrialists were hoping to make big money with the help of the accumulating *Sterling Balances*. The economic facts of life, however, were speaking a different language. Would the dreams nevertheless come true?

For the improvements in export policies to take effect, it was necessary to lift or change the import controls. At the end of March 1945 there was a talk between representatives of the India Office's *Economic and Overseas Department* and representatives of the Indian government's *Department for Development and Planning*, Sir Ardeshir Dalal and Iengar. Topic was 'the registration of post-war requirements of capital goods'. A change in procedure followed by the end of March 1945. A new list of *import licences* was published without considering the list of war-relevant goods. Indian importers were afraid of losing British goods. British industrialists showed no understanding for the delay in the 'post-war registration scheme for capital goods' and were angered by the delay in publishing the Indian *import licence*. Talks with Dalal and Iengar over the 'import licence of the post-war orders registered' showed that the *Chief Controller of Imports* carried out his policy of granting licences by orienting it to the volume of freight at hand, as was arranged with the government in Delhi for the period of the second quarter of 1945. Important for the British *Board of Trade* and the *Department of Overseas Trade* was to have an overall idea of needs in India for the post-war years. Information of this sort was given by Mr. Iengar.

In the spring of 1945, a delegation of Indian industrialists came to London. According to a memorandum on 4 May 1945, the India Office served as point of contact and intermediary between representatives of Indian business and representatives of the *Federation of British Industries*. goal of the Indian visitors in Great Britain was to get the British to promise deliveries of machines urgently needed in India for rebuilding the industrial strength of the country. The India Office itself did not participate directly in the talks, and the Indian delegates were not official representatives of the Indian government. The Indians negotiated with representatives of British business and then flew later to the United States, where they also wanted to talk to representatives of American business. According to Lord Listowel at the *Board of Trade* on 7 December 1944, A. H. Joyce assured A. F. Morley of the India Office's *Economic and Overseas Department* that the British government's export policy would allow the British free hand in the overseas export business. As usual, this was a matter for the British *Board of Trade* and the *Department of Overseas Trade*. This was an undertaking of great importance that involved the India Office and the Indian government in Delhi as well. The latter hoped that the Indian business delegation would see their visit to Great Britain as a contribution to rebuilding India.

In order to prepare for an intensification of Indo-British economic relations during this special visit of Indian industrialists, Sir Thomas Ainscough, the senior British Trade Commissioner, presented the *East India Association* in London a position paper on 27 February 1945 with the heading: **Britain's Indian Market - Past, Present and Future**. A hand-written note by Thomson of the India Office showed how the interests of British business had become blended into official British policy: *"It is interesting to see that the suggestions on the last page follow the line of thoughts of some of the bigger Export Companies."*

Ainscough, in his memorandum, pointed out that British exports would have to be increased by 50%, if Great Britain wanted to prevent a deterioration in its balance of payments and retain its pre-war standard of living. India had been Britain's export market for over 50 years. It was only in the decade before the war that India's British imports had been outstripped by South Africa and Australia. He wanted to know why India should not retake its position as most important export market for British goods. Close economic co-operation would be in the interest of both countries, despite the political differences - meaning here the constitutional considerations.

Another memorandum took up the problems in Indo-British economic relations for the post-war era. The Secretary of State for India interpreted the visit of eight Indian delegates as signalling good chances for the future of British export business in India. The minister encouraged the British to accept orders from Indian business. The minister's ulterior motive was to lessen the *Sterling Balances*. At the same time, he stressed India's traditional position in the British export business.

The Approaching Trip of Indian Industrialists

British export policy planned for the post-war period was explained by Lord Listowel on 7 December 1944, and also by the British Minister of Trade on 12 September 1944. The British government, especially the British Board of Trade, was interested in the volume of orders brought by the Indian delegation. This would enable the British to set their production capacities. On 15 January 1945, C.D. Birla wrote to Sir Akbar Hydari, the representative of India's official governmental delegation, before Hydari came on mission to London in March 1945. Birla listed the goods that absolutely had to be imported to India. His order was worth £25 million.

The British Board of Trade worked out export guidelines in August 1944 for the period after the war. Exports would have to be increased by 150% compared to 1942 or by 200% compared to pre-war levels. That would mean domestic markets would have to made less attractive and export markets more attractive for British business. The British Prime Minister accepted these guidelines.

On 11 December 1944, Lieschnigg of the Board of Trade wrote to Baxter and proposed that a *U. K. Industrial Commissioner* be set up in India. The commissioner's responsibility would be to establish contacts between Indian and British business persons. The proposal was rejected on the grounds that it would be *"dangerous for a British official to advise Indian industrialisation."* The British proposal came only after India had begun shaping its industrial policy. There were warnings about British nationalists who were not concerned with India's right of self-determination in economic matters and that these nationalists would put British economic interests at risk.

The British Treasury considered Indian inquiries, especial those about investment capital, as relating to British export policy in general. These were seen as an indication of how the *Sterling Balances* could be reduced by way of British exports to India. In this regard, Amery, the Secretary of State for India made a proposal. India's *Sterling Balances* deposited in London could be used as a means of paying for British exports to India. Keynes, who was working on drafts of a new order for the world economy and monetary policy with his American college White, rejected this absurd kind of solution.

It was desirable for the British side that the Indian government present a list of investments needed. The so-called *Hydari Circular* registered all export goods needed from Great Britain and industrialists' interest in British contacts.

Orders were collected at the India Office and passed on the Treasury and Ministry of Trade. The question of consumer goods production was handled by estimating pre-war consumption levels. Especially during the first few years after the war, the British government expected a reduction in the *Sterling Balances* by way of an increase in exports to India. The *Sterling Balances*, however, had become in the meantime a sort of surety for the Anglo-American *Lend-Lease* agreement.

In December 1945, the United States granted Great Britain $3.5 billion in credit. Great Britain owed India £1.2 billion. The Anglo-American agreement intended the credit not to be misused for paying off trade deficits. On the other hand, member nations of the *Sterling Area System* had 'frozen' sterling assets that were available to Great Britain for the redemption of credit. This was the political context in which the trip of Indian industrials stood. The trip to Great Britain and the United States had been announced by the Indian government on 10 October 1944 for the purpose of talks and negotiations over possible projects in the area of economic co-operation. Members of the delegation had the concrete task of analysing existing industrial production and the technical advantages of British and American industry, and studying the industrial economic plans of both nations for the post-war period. Members of the Indian delegation were: Mr. J.R.D. Tata, Mr. G.D. Birla, Mr. Nalini Ranjan Sarker, Mr. A.D. Shroff, Sir Sultan Chinoy, Mr. Laik Ali, Mr. Ajaib Singh.

The delegation came to London in the third week of May 1945 and stayed there for five weeks of consultations. The delegation then flew to the United States and held talks with representatives of American business. At the beginning of the second week of August, the delegation returned to Great Britain and finished talks by the end of the month. For lack of time, the delegation was not able to accept an invitation of the Canadian government, but one member of the delegation made a short stay in Ottawa and signed a contract with Canadian business representatives.

Weighing Up Advantages and Disadvantages of British or American Products

Without understanding the consequences of the British *sterling debt*, Indian business representatives asked about possibilities of raising funds. Domestic and foreign capital demand after the war made available capital more expensive, to unfavourable conditions for India. In the United States there was no possibility for the Indians to raise funds over a longer period of time; this was possible in Great Britain after a waiting period of up to two years.

Investment capital for power plants, heavy machinery, special machinery, transportation equipment, electrical equipment, mining equipment and chemical systems had a waiting period of two years in the United States and of over two years in Great Britain. Small machines and smaller special machines were cheaper in Great Britain than in the United States. American offers were at a fixed price, whereas British offers allowed for rising costs of raw materials and labour between reception of the offer and delivery.

In the context of India's political independence and in the context of the economic relations between Great Britain and India, the following can be observed:

Great Britain was suddenly confronted with the situation of having to accept India's independence and rapid industrialisation in the foreseeable future. British industrialists were doing everything to adjust to this new situation. The technical and industrial potential of Western industrial nations inspired the Indian delegation. At the end of the 'promotion tour' the delegation had the impression that the American standard was superior to that of the British.

Did this result in Indian businesses ordering more products from the United States? Or was there a reason to be found in the massive indebtedness of the Indian economy in buying and building numerous prestige projects?

To what extent did the *Balance of Payments* and the *Sterling Balances* play a decisive role in India's growing indebtedness? And that the World Bank and the *International Monetary Fund* forced India to take on credit? Was India forced to do this because the United States and Great Britain were not willing to make the 'frozen' sterling assets in the *Bank of England* available for financing India's economic rebuilding?

Reactions to the Indian Business Delegation's Trip to London

The exploratory trip of Indian industrialists did not have to wait for commentary, neither from the members themselves nor their critics.

The first reaction to the official report of the *promotion tour* came from G.D. Birla.

G.D. Birla presented his impression in the *Industrialist's Mission*. He noted that Great Britain had shorter delivery times than the United States. It was a fact that Great Britain had India's sterling assets at its disposal and was thus able to process transactions more quickly and easily. The United States countered by demanding that the British government pay off its *sterling debts* to creditor nations of the Empire or the Commonwealth. The American demand was the condition for giving Great Britain short-term or long-term credit. The United States secured for itself in this way a potential 'buyer strata' that was transferring sterling into the common *Empire-Dollar-Pool*. One critical voice warned about the hasty purchasing behaviour of Indian businesses and of the Indian delegation in London and in the United States. The *Manchester Guardian* drew attention to the Indian demand for economic self-determination.

The *Eastern Economist* reported on the visit of the Indian delegation in Great Britain. The delegation visited numerous industrial plants in Birmingham and Manchester: *ICI Dyestuffs and Plastics; Metropolitan Vickers; Courtaulds; Lever Brothers.* British business supported the Indian delegation in desiring the industrialisation of their country and agreed also with their political views. Among other things, this meant the 'Indianisation' of new businesses. An example of this was the **Birla-Nuffield Agreement**, that was enacted without British financial participation, but made use of British technical advice and British patents. British industrialists believed that they were to play a roll in the economic rebuilding of India. However, there was a hurdle for British investors interested in India. The British Treasury prohibited larger investments in foreign countries; any outpouring of important currency reserves had to be prevented. Britain's balance of payments was endangered and its balance of trade unfavourable. Some British investors were also frightened away by the political changes in India. Thus, the opinion of the*Eastern Economist*.

Gandhi's Reaction to the Delegation's Trip.

On 7 May 1945, Gandhi gave his opinion about the delegation's trip to London and the United States. Asked about his views on the plans to develop Indian industry, Gandhi said:

"Big merchants, capitalists, industrialists and others, speak and write against the Government, but in action...will, and even profit through it. The bright spot of the situation, however, is that all big interests proclaim with one voice that India wants nothing less than her own elected National Government to shape her destiny free of all control, british or any other."

Gandhi favoured small, self-sufficient, decentralised economic units. *"This independence will come only when interests big and small are prepared to forego the crumbs that fall to them from partnership with the British in the loot which British rule takes from India."*

Gandhi called for British withdrawal from the internal affairs of India and the 'transfer of power' to the indigenous elite.

"Verbal protests will count for nothing so long as this partnership continues unchecked. The so-called unofficial delegation dare not proceed, whether for inspection or for entering into a shameful deal so long as the moving spirits of the congress working committee have been detained without any trial for the sole crime of sincerely striving for India's independence and without shedding a drop of blood except their own."

In a dance of conflicting opinions, Tata, who in many respects represented different economic views, replied to Gandhi. Tata was one of the co-authors of the £75 million Bombay-Plan and member of the delegation to Great Britain and the United States. He felt insulted by Gandhi's remarks.

"I emphatically repudiate the suggestion that in visiting Britain and America for the purpose of investigating the difficult problems with which Indian industry is faced at this critical juncture, we are out to enter into shameful deals behind the country's back. Object of visit: to survey the economy and the industrial developments which have taken place in those countries since the war, and

acquire for them such knowledge as will enable us better to play our part in the future economic development of the country."

Likewise, Birla felt compelled to react to Gandhi's statement: *"I refuse to believe that you could give public expression to your distrust of the bona fides of myself and Mr. Tata and Mr. Kasturbhai Lalbhai. We know our limitations and know we have no authority to enter even into a good deal, to say nothing of a shameful one. Your statement is sure to be construed as a strong denunciation of our motives."*

In this conflict, Gandhi responded that his comment assumed a hypothetical case and that it was not a hasty expression of opinion. Gandhi contradicted the apparent Indian interests of the industrialists and found them guilty of deliberate agitating for their own ends. What Gandhi was criticising became apparent in Birla's co-operation with the India Office in the sector of aeroplane production that had taken an exceptional position during the war.

Amery, the Secretary of State for India, wrote to Viscount Swinton on 30 April 1945 and mentioned the co-operation with Tata and Shroff, members of the Indian business delegation to Great Britain. Tata was interested in building an 'Indian Air Line' and was chairman of *Tata Sons Ltd.* A.D. Shroff was director of a number of industrial concerns, some also in the Tata group. The explanation reflects Tata's important role and influence in India. The India Office did not possess any air transportation plans for the post-war period, but Amery did not doubt that the India Office would have an important part in the company that was to be founded. The Tata group had already worked for the military side of war-goods deliveries to India, namely, for the Royal Air Force.

After the end of the war, *Tata Ltd.* Tried to build up an 'aircraft manufacturing industry' with the support of the India Office. Another member of the delegation, Sir Sultan Chinoy, who was interested in building up an automobile industry in India, also showed interest in a possible aircraft manufacturing industry. These examples show clearly the entanglement of British politics in Indian business after the war.

After the delegation of Indian industrialists visited London in 1945, a business delegation from the Indian Principalities visited Great Britain in 1946. They wished to cement their economic ties with the British in the post-war period and defend sovereign economic privileges in the face of a future unified and independent India.

The theory can be presented, that the Indian Principalities appeared in London as competition to the Indian industrialists. This competition was promoted by the

British government, as 40% of India's economic power lay in the hands of the principalities. This was reason enough, after achieving formal recognition of independence on 15 August 1947, for Nehru's pressure on principalities resisting being included in the newly created union, especially Hyderabad, Travancore and Kaschmir.

But first the constitutional problem in India had to be clarified, and there were no doubts that Lord Wavell, the Viceroy, was capable of doing this.

BUSINESS DELEGATION OF THE INDIAN PRINCIPALITIES

On 6 March 1946, the *Department of Overseas Trade* announced that a business delegation from the Principality Hyderabad was being sent to London. A trip by representatives of the Indian principalities had been planned for the year 1945, but not carried out. On 20 December 1945, the Manchester Guardian reported about the approaching visit of a 'trade delegation' in London.

The Indian principalities accounted for 40% of economic production of the Indian subcontinent, but received only somewhat more than 4% of investments in India. The principalities were afraid of the future at the end of the war; the continuing restrictions that the British had set up in 1939 under the *Defence of India Rules* lowered chances of economic development. Transfer of capital had become more difficult, and the principalities welcomed any change in the rules the British dictated. Reproached for having low tax rates, representatives of the principalities answered, in the direction of India, by pointing to even lower tax rates in the United States. The Minister of Trade in Indore, Captain Dhanda, justified tax policies by stating that the principalities needed them to raise the living standards of their people. The delegates from the principalities gave their purchasing list to the *Board of Trade* and the *Federation of British Industries*. On the list were industrial installations, machinery, machine parts, electrical equipment, paper products, cotton textiles, wool products, silver goods, leather goods, dyes, plastic products, medicine and chemical works.

During the war, the principalities had fought along the side of the British and its allies and had been able to observe the technical development of the West. The principalities hoped to be able to accomplish their plans for development after the war with the help of British investments, as is expressed in the *Statement of Government of India's Industrial Policy*, published in India on 23 April 1945: *"Licensing Board should have a directive to the effect that the existing backward position of the Indian States in the matter of industrial development must be recognized and that favourable treatment must be accorded to industrial proposals emanating from Indian States."*

The principalities were aiming for economic co-operation with Great Britain. Close co-operation with India was also aimed for in order to influence the financial and economic policies of the Indian government. The economic and financial policies of the Indian princes found a response in an article by Charles Graves, *The Ruling Princes of India.*

Graves' newspaper article was about the position of the Indian princes in the British web of power in India, the status of the 'resident', the British representative at the prince's court, economic power and potential, and the political and economical connections with other Indian principalities. Pressured by the British, a number of smaller principalities had to merge as confederations. The principalities wanted closer ties to Great Britain. This wish was not exclusively in their own interest, but was also to be seen in the larger context of a 'self-governing India'. Economic co-operation would also strengthen the political bonds between Great Britain and India after independence, as Graves continued. An immediate result of the delegation of the Indian Princes was the setting up of a *Trade Commissioner of the Principalities* in London, at the initiative of the Principality of Travancore. The delegation backed up its decision with the Indian government's announcement of good Indo-British co-operation. However, the *Federation of British Industries* was not inclined to receive the delegation. On 7 September, the *Political Department* at the India Office announced the names of those delegates whose trip was being postponed until March 1945.

The delegation was made up of the Prime Minister of Patiala, Mr. Malik, the Industrial Adviser of Bhopal, Abdul Rehman Siddiqui, Mr E. Christensen, cement expert and industrial leader in Kathiawar, and Mir Maqbool Mahmood. The *High Commissioner for India* and representatives of the *Federation of British Industries* were to lead talks with the delegation. On 13 March 1946, a *Chatham House* paper was discussed by Mir Maqbool Mahmood, Secretary of the *Chancellor of the Chamber of Princes*, Sir George Nelson, President of the *Federation of British Industries* and his deputy, Mr. Moir Mackenzie. An important result was that a public relations office should be planned for London with a general agent representing all of India.

In the course of the trip by the Indian Princes' delegation to Great Britain and to the United States, those two countries began wrestling over influence in South Asia. During the Second World War India's trade network shifted to the disadvantage of Great Britain and to the advantage of the United States. The *Lend-Lease* agreement and allied deliveries of raw materials raised the pressure of competition on the subcontinent, and this did not remain without consequences for the economical and financial situation of the British at the end of the war.

4.2. Competing Trade Partners: Great Britain and the United States Search for the Export Market of the Future in South Asia

Object of competition between Great Britain and the United States was the rising demand for basic industrial industries, such as heavy industry, iron and steel production and mining.

The United States expanded its trading with India during the war and achieved a trade surplus with that country. Indian exports to the United States increased compared to the period before the war. In Indian import trade, the United States surpassed Great Britain in 1951 with Rs. 1674 Lakhs to Rs. 1192 Lakhs. In 1946 Great Britain still exercised import and export controls and used these instruments to prevent uncontrolled trading.

How was, this not withstanding, the trading business possible?

During the war, economic relations between the United States and India were determined by the needs of war. Growing dependency of the British on American credit, the stationing of American troops in South Asia, the establishing of American information centres and the mediating mission of Johnson, the American special envoy strengthened the political and the economic influence of the United States in India.

Trade between India and the United States rested to a large degree on the basis of *Lend-Lease*, as was made possible by the Anglo-American agreement in 1942. Up until 1 July 1945, the United States exported goods worth $2,128,803,000 to India, of which munitions and other war deliveries made up $1,288,498,000. The rest consisted of petrochemical products worth $161,721,000, industrial goods for $494,673,000, and agrarian products worth $183,911,000. In return, India exported rubber, tea, magnesium and other raw materials to the United States.

Deliveries were made on a credit basis and at prices far under Indian market value. Indian deliveries to the United States on the basis of the *Lend-Lease* agreement raised inflation in India and destroyed the functioning of the Indian economy for domestic supplies and for deliveries to Great Britain as well.

In 1946 India was forced to cancel $45 million in US debts to offset deliveries on the basis of *Lend-Lease*. The Indian government had to, according to contract, give back 226 million ounces of silver that were used as means of payment under *Lend-Lease*. A further result of the agreement was that an independent India owed the United States $178,405,648 on 31 March 1949. With this settlement, the United States achieved the total redemption of $146,472,000 worth of imports from India to the United States in 1945. Compared to the trade balance in 1937/38, when the United States had 7.5% of Indian imports and 10.1% of Indian exports, the balance changed to India's disfavour in 1944/45. The US share of Indian imports went up to 25.7%, and the US share of Indian exports up to only 21.2%; this meant a doubling of export share, but more than a tripling of import share, seen from the Indian point of view. Compared to trading with the United States, Indian trading with Great Britain remained relatively unchanged.

In spite of the trading with the USA during the war by way of delivering important raw materials for the machinery of war, India at independence was faced with a mountain of debt. The Indian government normally was not permitted to sign international treaties, but had closed a settlement with the United States.

An assertion can be made on the basis of this: The politically motivated support by the United States of the Indian struggle for freedom and of the Indian independence movement only served to secure a market for American business. The United States reached its goal by settling with India and turning a British creditor before independence into a debtor of the United States after independence.

The advantages for Great Britain lay in postponing payment of British debt in India until 1952 by way of financial moratorium. British debt to the United States remained postponed while the United States had access to the Indian market, as India disposed over large dollar reserves.

Great Britain had to make more and more concessions to American interests, since it was caught up in financial entanglements and could not, without the help of the USA, revitalise its fallow economy. The financial dependency of Great Britain was a result of the conditions of the Anglo-American financial agreement of December 1945. The agreement contained, among other things, a warning to Great Britain to repay British *sterling debts* or to make a settlement with its creditor nations.

Was a trade-off perhaps the basis of negotiating the Indo-British *Financial Agreement* of 14 August 1947 – Indian independence for liquidating British debts?

The result of British debt to the United States was enlarged American control of the Indian market and of the Indian economy. Great Britain's economy was not in a position to fill India's import demand. Both the British government and British business were far more involved in paying back American credit than was supposed before signing the agreement. The United States took advantage of the financial commitments of the British and intervened in the Indian market. A letter of the American trade representative in India recommended taking up contact with Pandit Nehru, just after he was appointed director of the Indian transitional government's Ministry of Trade. The American trade representative was to discuss a catalogue of American business interests with Nehru.

What was Nehru's role in this? Did he collaborate with Western powers and business persons?

An example here is the establishing of a *Joint Mica Mission*. Representatives of Great Britain and of the United States, three from each country controlled the entire production. Indian criticism did not remain silent. Nonetheless, the power of big business in the US and in the UK dominated political life.

American-Indian co-operation manifested itself in numerous sectors of business in the form of *joint ventures*.

In the **automobile** sector, Birlas Hindustan Motors signed an agreement with Studebaker Corporation; Walchand Hirachand's Premier Automobiles with Chrysler Corporation; Motor House (Gujerat) Ltd. with Kaiser-Frazer Export Corporation.

In the sector of **radio and electronic devices,** Fazalbhoy Photophone Equipment Company co-operated with Radio Corporation of America.

In the sector of **rayon** as a substitute for cotton, the National Rayon Corporation, founded by Sir Purushottamdas Thakurdas, Sir Ardeshir Dalal, A.D. Shroff and Walchand Hirachand, co-operated with the Skenanda Rayon Corporation of Utica, New York and Lockwood, Greene and Company of New York.

The Indian side took the view that it was better to negotiate and sign contracts with American companies because better conditions could be expected. Unfortunately, the Indians did not feel they were treated as equals. The *Eastern Economist* reported on 16 November 1945:

"The terms offered by India are not such as to appeal to the majority of American investors...they feel that unless they have a voice in the production, accounting, product standards and marketing methods, their participation would not be readily forthcoming."

Rayon could serve as an example. This was new territory for Indian business. Americans would only do business if the Indians agreed to conditions such as paying Rs. 4.0 million for technical support without procurement of materials. The Indian side had to provide Rs. 11.0 million in wages and Rs. 1.25 million in royalties per year for a contractual period of ten years.

The British point of view of the Indo-American joint ventures was presented by Sir Nelson, the President of the *Federation of British Industries* on 21 March 1945. The members of the British business association were concerned about their economic influence in the changing Empire of the post-war period. Sir Nelson spoke on the topic *The British Commonwealth in Relation to the Great Economic Units of the World.* Commonwealth members had a right to economic development through the aid of other Commonwealth nations.

More moderate and tempered is the personal impression of the delegate Mir Maqbool Mahmood from his trip to the United States in March 1945.

1. He called for closer co-operation between the United States and the British Empire in the political and economic sectors.
2. He called for more co-operation within the British Empire.
3. Discussing India's economic strength would be a good possibility for clarifying the open constitutional question of India.

At the end of the First World War, contact had taken up by American industry and American finance with India. British industrialists and bankers had followed this penetration with distrust. They answered with an embargo against credit from American banks and institutions, and with strengthening the establishment of the British *Managing Agency Houses* in India.

A strengthening of the roll of the USA in India originated in passages of the Anglo-American trade agreement of 1938.

"You will remember that in article 4 of the Indo-U.K. trade agreement of 1939 H.M.G. re-affirmed their undertaking to maintain the preference at its present rate (of about 2s/ per lb.) until 19 August 1942, and that in the note which appears at the end of schedule I of the U.K.-U.S.A. Trade Agreement of 1938 the U.K. had previously promised the Americans that she would be prepared before decisions are taken as to the level of the preference after August 1942 to examine the position as it then stands and the possibility of reducing the margin of preference and that meanwhile it would not be increased."

There certainly was a danger of the principalities doing business together with the USA without the consent of the British government. Rumbold wrote to Baxter and Croft on 29 November 1946 and referred to the co-operation between Indore and the United States; Rumbold proposed that the central Indian government assert its influence. In view of the coming constitutional changes in India, he pointed out the danger of the Indian principalities becoming economically independent. In order to keep British business from being helplessly surrendered to American competition, Baxter at the India Office proposed informing the

Board of Trade and the *Export Promotion Department*, responsible for British exporting. British trade representatives in India then travelled with representatives of the British export lobby to Indore to promote the buying of British products.

The British *Trade Commissioner* in India viewed *Lend-Lease* and the consequences of this agreement as the cause of increased American competition. American aid during the war and the interest of the American export business in the Indian market after the war were upsetting British trade policy. After the First World War, India had had good experience with American export policy. The British predicted an increase in sales of American goods for railway construction, automobile production, aircraft construction and the building of roads. Representatives of British export business were relieved to see that British suppliers were offering their products at lower prices than the Americans, and that this would make the British more competitive.

Indo-British economic relations after the Second World War were concentrated on Britain and India co-operating with each other; on the other hand, the Anglo-American financial agreement of December 1945 had an effect on these economic relations. Furthermore, plans for a new trade agreement after the end of the war affected the nature of these economic relations. Not least the political component, the undecided constitutional question of an independent India in the future, complicated previous Indo-British relations. During the Second World War these relations were conditioned by an external threat, which meant giving the British a relatively free hand for effecting required emergency measures that were often also supported by the executive branch of the US government. In the further course of events, the political demands of the Indians collided with the interests of the British business lobby in India. The situation was made even more critical by the British government's difficulties in finding a solution after the war to its debts both to Empire creditors and to the United States.

5 Indo-British Economic Relations after the End of the Second World War

Outline of the Political and Economic Situation

In the final phase of the Second World War the British economy was subjected to strong pressure by the Americans. At the end of the war, British business was worried about its status in India.

The constitutional question for India was avoided for the duration of the war. The *Cripps Mission* failed in 1942. The political demands of the Indian independence movement were postponed until after the war. After the war, the constitutional question became more and more the focus of attention in political and economic matters. With the accumulation of Indian sterling assets in the *Bank of England* in London, the economic and financial position of India in the Commonwealth improved. At the same time, however, the economic and financial position of Great Britain was deteriorating. Great Britain, victor in the ranks of the allies, was becoming more and more the loser in the struggle for economic and political power.

Problems of all sorts – supply bottlenecks in England itself, debts to its colonies and to the United States, supply problems in India, transfer of money and personnel to occupied Germany – limited the ability of the British government to manoeuvre. Elections for the lower house of Parliament brought a change in government. *Labour* by itself, after 20 years of either opposition or coalition, ran the government. The British expected the new government to solve the difficult structural problems with the economy. The Indians expected a solution to the Indian constitutional question and repayment of the British *sterling debt*. During these days of changing expectations, a delegation of the Indian government, the so called *Hydari Mission*, travelled to London at the beginning of March 1945 to negotiate with the British government. Topic of negotiations was to be deliveries of the minimum amount of necessary consumer goods, as the British government had promised India for the time after the war. During the war, India had been forced by import and export bans and by currency and financial controls to do more or less without consumer goods, and its production capacities had been transformed for wartime production.

The Hydari Mission reported that the British government had agreed to an increase in trading volume starting in 1945. Great Britain promised an increase of £19.0 million in exports of consumer goods and supplementary raw materials for the year 1945, and an increase of £17.0 million for the year 1946. The increase in exports was only possible by relaxing Article Seven of the *Open General Licence* in March 1945, and by lifting British export controls for numerous export articles.

Which export articles were sent to India?

Great Britain sent radios, motorcycles, buses and automobiles to India. During the war, General Motors, the American competitor, tried to help the Indians build up the automobile industry in India. After lifting the export controls, there was still an obstacle for delivering British goods to India. Shipping capacities were limited after the war. The Indian government demanded that the British government make compensatory deliveries for goods delivered to the allied military during the war. Produced and delivered were:

- 300,000 tons of steel (total production in India: 900,000 tons)
- 1.2 million military boots (total production: 3.0 million)
- 500,000 tons of timber (total production: 1.0 million tons)
- 40% of wool textiles produced in India
- 600,000 tons of cement (total production: 2.1 million tons)
- 800,000 yards of cotton textiles (total production: 1.4 million yards)

For military goods, India allowed price discounts totalling £3.0 million in 1945 and £27.0 million in 1946. Its deficit fell from £210 million in 1945 to £147 million in 1946.

For the first time in the political development of colonial India, the circumstances affecting negotiations had changed, and this helped the Hydari Mission. Representatives of the Indian government met directly with their colleagues in the British government, without the mediation of "any intermediate Department machinery". This development was expressly welcomed by the Secretary of State for India. Nonetheless, the demands listed by the Hydari Mission could only be partly satisfied.

Not only productive economic power had changed in India during the course of the war. The rise in export quotas in allied countries because of the war was also accompanied by a rise in currency holdings. India as creditor to Great Britain must also be seen in this context. India reduced its pre-war *sterling debt* in Great Britain during the war, and went on to accumulate sterling assets in London. These assets totalled £1.1 billion by the end of the war. Great Britain was left with the problem of paying off these debts. What could be thus more obvious than co-operating economically with India in the post-war period. In 1943, the Indian Minister of Finance proposed placing this money in a 'reconstruction fund', an international reconstruction programme for India led by the British government. The fund was to ensure that basic needs of the population would be met.

During the war, the British government had called for the participation of British business in the development of the Indian economy. British business persons had been urged during the war to make contacts with Indians after the war.

Nonetheless, the latest export limits issued on 5 July 1945 must have appeared as virtual export barriers to the initiatives of the British export business.

Predictions for and difficulties in Indian industrial development were analysed and published by the *Indian Research Group* after the war. This was a group of British economists working for the government in Delhi and developing expertise for the economic problems and for the economic framework of the post-war period. The results of studies were also sent to the India Office in London, which forwarded them to the press and other interested parties.

Material published analysed the economy in 1939 and how it changed during the Second World War. Two large sectors of business were designated as growth areas for India after the war: jute and cotton.

As previously mentioned, the British were afraid of having American competition on the Indian subcontinent, especially after the highly-probable achievement of Indian independence in the foreseeable future. For their own protection, British businesses were making trading and business agreements with their Indian partners. Despite, or perhaps because of the debts to the United States and India, the British carried on working on Indo-British economic relations. The Empire's economic block was supposed to become established as a 'third block' next to the developing political blocks of the USA and the USSR.

5.1. Indo-British Co-Operation (Birla-Nuffield Agreement)

The *Open General Licence No. 7* was issued on 2 March 1945 to prepare the way for expanding exports and meeting, in part, the demand for consumer goods. Especially permitted was the exporting of industrial equipment and machinery. The legal groundwork was set down in *section 6(4) and 12(2)*. The British Board of Trade had established a new policy setting exporters free to look for and find individual export markets. The Board of Trade analysed export possibilities with respect to the entire export programmes of individual companies and checked the supply of the domestic market with potential export products.

There seemed to be nothing in the way of Indo-British co-operation. However, on 11 June and 5 July 1945, export controls were suddenly stiffened, and this had a crippling effect on the desired export initiative. The uncertainty as to the length of the war in the Far East and the shortage of currency reserves brought an unexpected end to the visions of Indian industrialists and British exporters.

What kind of economic co-operation did Great Britain have with all of India? With the principalities? With India?

The co-operation with the principalities was as follows: The willingness of the Indian principalities to co-operate with Great Britain was a further step in the development of overall Indo-British economic co-operation. Many of the principalities were willing to offer wartime help to the *Paramountcy Power* during the Second World War. At the end of the war, a delegation of princes met on 28 September 1945 with Viceroy Wavell for further talks. The first talk on economic co-operation had taken place a year previously in September 1944. One topic for discussion was setting down the rights of the principalities in a new trading agreement, and another was working out an arrangement with the British government that included economic development and all other relevant political issues. Liaison groups were set up to co-ordinate and check the co-operation. At this point, the princes had been conceded sovereignty after a possible British withdrawal from India. For their own part, the principalities did not want to block the constitutional development of India.

The princes warned of the dangers when they would no longer possess the strong economic position in India as previously. They saw the validity of bilateral agreements, the security and political integrity of their states endangered. Wavell took care in his comments to dispel the worries of the Indian princes. Here following are a number of examples to illustrate the co-operation.

A project shared by the British with the Indian principalities was the *Hydro-Electric projects for Indian states*. The project was set up on 12 November 1945 between Great Britain and the principalities Mysore, Kashmir, Travancore, Madras, Hyderabad, Gwalior, Indore, Jaipur, Udaipur, Kotah and Cochin.

Just before India's independence, Great Britain attempted to sign economic co-operation agreements with the independent principalities. Tranvancore, with an abundance of raw materials, signed an agreement with the British firm *British Thorium Ltd.* arranging delivery of thorium and other raw materials. Travancore, like the principality Hyderabad, had set up a trade representative in London, a so-called *Agent General*.

The principalities Baroda, Mysore and Hyderabad made economic co-operation agreements with British-India in order to influence British-Indian fiscal policy. The principalities expected Great Britain to support Indian industry in rebuilding business.

At almost the same time, on 23 April 1945, the Indian central government issued a *Statement of Government of India's Industrial Policy*. In this the government announced:

- the placing of various key industries under central control of the state
- the fiscal policy of the central government in Delhi
- financial participation of the central government in rebuilding industry
- the licensing and approval of various branches of industry
- other control measures

To support the government's initiative, Sir Ardeshir Dalal toured the Indian provinces and Indian principalities in his capacity as Minister of Planning and Development. He strove to promote the central government's economic plan. The free development of Indian industry and Indo-British trade relations was hindered by the larger-scaled trading carried on by the UKCC. The British Minister of Trade used the UKCC as 'permanent trading organisation'. The minister wanted to see that the UKCC was covering the risks of smaller British businesses in India.

Indo-British economic relations were assessed as generally good by the *Globereuter Eastern*. This favoured the so-called *Birla-Nuffield Agreement* that was signed on 20 June 1945. Preliminary talks had been held near the end of the war. A meeting between G.D. Birla and representatives of the Nuffield Organisation settled the particulars of an exchange programme for British technicians and Indian trainees. The plan foresaw training Indian workers in the period of time from 1945 to 1948. British industrialists saw this agreement as a prophylactic measure to push back the expansion of American competition on the Indian subcontinent. For a number of British business sectors this was a realistic chance to increase sales on the Indian market.

The textile business hoped for a major expansion of quality clothing articles in India. Textile manufacturers in Lancashire planned expanding their offering of fashionable wear for higher-income groups in India.

The automobile industry, first and foremost *Nuffield Motors Company*, invested Rs. 4 Crores with the help of Birla in an assembly plant for *Morris Cars*. Technicians from Great Britain took up work in India immediately after the contract was closed.

The radio and electronics business in Britain worked out plans for producing radio sets and other electronic goods, after analysing potential consumer groups. This undertaking was almost undone by the enormously high import duties of India and the customs policy of the government in Delhi. The government relented by reducing its import duties and expanding the list of the *Open General Licence*.

Producing artificial fertiliser for India's expanding agrarian business was the envisioned by *Imperial Chemical Industries Ltd.* The company planned three factories for the production of ammonia sulphate at a rate of 350,000 tons of sulphate per year.

Tractors Ltd. London was involved in talks about covering the need for machinery on the Indian market.

Makers of porcelain and earthenware saw good sales chances for their products in India if the Indian government would loosen its import regulations.

Subject of following inquiry, in addition to the willingness to economic co-operation, will be the effects of the Anglo-American Financial Agreement on Indo-British economic relations in the post-war period.

5.2. Anglo-American Financial Agreement

With the end of hostilities in Europe in May 1945 and in the Far East in August 1945, Great Britain was faced with facts of financial and monetary policies that led to the rapid end of political rule in India and subsequently to further de-colonisation in Great Britain's African and Asian possessions. The Labour government was confronted with practically insurmountable problems: unstable political conditions in India, indebtedness to numerous sterling-creditor nations, and the desire of many British for a 'welfare state'. Great Britain's wartime debt to the United States culminated in the *Loan Agreement* of December 1945. The loss of the imperial preferences, encrusted economic structures and the failure to make structural adjustments, that is, technical innovation, were taking their toll.

How did the *Anglo-American Financial Agreement* come about?

At the end of the war, Great Britain had debts totalling £3355 billion. Export volumes would have to be increased by at least 50% in order to reach pre-war levels. Shipping tonnage in export trade decreased in the course of the war from 22.1 to 15.9 million tons. Great Britain would have needed three to five years to come up with via exports the necessary sum of money to pay off this debt. But the economy, totally restructured for wartime production, was not capable of this in 1945. The British asked the United States for a £1250 billion loan. This was the equivalent of $3750 billion. Goods had to be purchased using dollars, and, of the dollar-block, only the United States came into consideration as potential creditor. Great Britain received the loan to especially favourable conditions, 2% interest over 50 years beginning in 1951. Most important goal for Great Britain was to reduce the *Sterling Balances*. It was the British government's additional responsibility to achieve convertibility for the *Pound Sterling* by July 1947 at the latest, as agreed in the Anglo-American Financial Agreement of 1945 and, earlier, in the *Bretton Woods Agreement* of 1944.

With the Great Depression in mind, the British government was particularly concerned about the danger of another American economic crisis that would make repayment of the loan very difficult. Criticism was raised against the *financial agreement*, but the British government had to accept the conditions of the agreement. These conditions also had consequences for the financial relations to India. Subsequent to the agreement with the United States, Britain reached a *financial agreement* with India. Britain lost some of its belief in the new international institutions that were to give wings to free global trading. The *International Trade Organisation* (ITO) had just been established in December 1945, as planned at Bretton Woods. GATT, *General Agreement on Tariffs and Trade*, an agreement to reduce custom duties and limits, was only slowly ratified and did not become binding until 1948. The International Monetary Fund (IMF) only disposed at first over insufficient margins of credit; there were not enough potential creditors available. That meant that it was absolutely necessary for the British to obtain the money required for repaying the credit by way of export trading. On top of this, the USA got rid of a troublesome trading competitor in the Far East by issuing this credit to Great Britain. The high demand for US-dollars and exporting carried out on the basis of the dollar during the war lessened the volume of available dollars in the post-war period. The relevance of this would become clear during the course of negotiations between the British and the Indians in the years 1946 and 1947.

Ratification of the Anglo-American *Financial Agreement* by the American Congress came despite fierce resistance on the part of a number of congress members. What made ratification of the agreement possible was the political idea espoused in Congress of using Great Britain as a 'bulwark' against the advance of the Soviet Union in Eastern Europe. This included weakening the political Left in Britain and slowing down the nationalisation of British industry. On a global scale, Congress was pursuing the policy of strengthening and opening up free trade, and removing protectionist trading barriers and the imperial customs preferences. Additional priorities were dissolving the *Empire-Dollar-Pool* and reducing the sterling assets accumulation of British creditors in London.

5.3. Constitutional Issues and Reflections on a New Trade Agreement after the End of the War

The Anglo-American Financial Agreement improved Great Britain's economic situation by adding a $3.5 billion credit, but it made the paying off of *sterling debts* more difficult to Empire countries, among others India and Egypt. Another difficulty was the *business lobby* and its interests in India.

How could these problems be solved?

The United States insisted on repayment of debts. The USA was the leading economic power after the war. *UNRRA* and *Marshall Aid* were only made possible by the economic power of the United States. Great Britain had to bow to the dictates of the USA. The only left was to manoeuvre countries such as India that were subordinated to Great Britain to the financial advantage of the British. One possibility was to 'exchange' the *sterling debts* for the renouncing of the constitutional privileges of the British in economic matters. This could be for the transition period or also by way of a new constitution without such discriminating articles as those in the constitution of 1935. Is this the reason why India agreed to disfavourable results in the *Sterling Balances Negotiations*? Unfortunately, it is not possible to find an exact explanation for India's agreement in these negotiations. The assumption remains that there could have been a logical connection between the constitutional questions and the negotiations over a new commercial agreement.

The British government made concessions in the constitutional question to the Indian side, to the disadvantage of the *British-business interests-lobby* in London. The lobby's *Joint Committee on India* put pressure on the British government to protect British interests in India after independence by way of a constitutional guarantee. India achieved a compromise with the British government in the negotiations over the *Sterling Balances*. The Indo-British *Financial Agreement* signed on 14 August 1947 could serve as evidence for the argument stated above. The *Financial Agreement* provided for a debt reduction in the form of a moratorium. The agreement was to be binding until 14 February 1948, at which time it was to be re-negotiated. The text of the agreement, worked out in December 1947, and its ratification in February 1948 prolonged the agreement automatically each year until 1952.

After clarifying the financial situation, it was time to shape a new Indo-British trade agreement.

Discussions up to this point had been focused on the expected volume of trading and what an agreement of this kind would be worth. British business had a considerable volume of trade in India after the Second World War. The exact volume of business with India was never precisely calculated. The India Office estimated it between £300 million and £2.0 billion. It was a lucrative market for the weak British export business. During the *transition period*, the last thing the India Office wanted to do was to force the Indian government to sign a trade agreement, even though the USA had signed one with India.

Nevertheless, the British government had worked out a draft for an agreement on 23 April 1947, just in case. This was to let the Indians know in a diplomatic way that *"greater readiness of Indians to recognise their dependence on the U.K. in connection with India's economic development"* would be necessary. The British government hoped that India after independence would remain in the *Commonwealth* because of the *Empire-Dollar-Pool* and the *Sterling Area.* Britain expected to carry out negotiations over a trade agreement parallel to negotiations over the *transfer of power*. Great Britain did not want any of its economic interests subject to an area outside jurisdiction.

Demands to link the *transfer of power* to negotiations over a trade agreement became more concrete as the transfer date approached. The India Office was besieged more and more by representatives of the British-business lobby and politically harassed. The India Office analysed the political situation in India and concluded that an Indian transitional government could remain longer than a year in office, that is until 1948, without changing the discriminating articles in the *Government of India Act, 1935*. Viceroy Wavell wrote to Pethick-Lawrence, the Secretary of State for India, and complained that the discriminating articles in the *Government of India Act* were a burden in the negotiations over a new trade agreement.

Numerous plans for a Indo-British trade agreement are summarised below. A memorandum was sent from Trunbull to Donalson and Rumbold on 14 March 1947 explaining how the existing trade agreement could be changed into a commercial treaty. The Finance Department at the India Office had made a proposal on 4 November 1946 for a Indo-British commercial treaty from the perspective of finances, that is, from the perspective of India's sterling assets in London.

The *sterling debts*, originally accumulated by Britain's Secretary of State for India, occupied an especially important position. Not only the *Government of India Act, 1935*, but also other laws, such as the *East India Loans Act, 1937*, made the Secretary of State for India directly responsible to the creditors. The laws regulated repayment and interest as well as the administration of assets. The *Sterling Balances* are a strange story in Indo-British relations.

It did not seem to be politically the right moment to return to the negotiating level of Sir S. Cripps in 1942. Cripps proposed that Britain should first sign a commercial treaty with British-India's successor states and then to negotiate the pending political treaty. Linking a commercial treaty with the agreement to the *transfer of power* would have caused political unrest in India. In an anouncement on 19 November 1946 by the British government via the Viceroy, the treaty agreement of both parties India and Great Britain was laid down. The ministers and departments responsible for making the agreement were given the task of deciding what consequences the negotiations might have and what possibility there was of reaching agreement.

6 Indo-British Economic Relations before Independence of India

Indo-British economic relations before the announcement of independence were marked by various problems:

- The problem of Indian import policies and the cancelling of existing import licences by 30 June 1947.
  On the one hand there was the Indian desire of British imports to keep the black market from growing. At the same time danger of inflation was to be avoided. The cancelling of import licences was planned for the first half of 1947. The resulting problem was to co-ordinate import and export policies as well as currency controls linked to these policies.
- The future of the British economy and British trading in and with India was unclear.
- Negotiations for a new commercial treaty between Great Britain and India were approaching.
- The practicality of British trade guaranties in the *Government of India Act, 1935* had to be reviewed in light of negotiations over the *transfer of power*.
- The *Joint Committee on India* increased its influence on day-to-day politics as the *transfer of power* approached.
- The British government had to have a settlement or a repayment plan worked out by July 1947 for the *Sterling Balances* in order to fulfill the stipulations of the Anglo-American Financial Agreement.

In light of British business interests in India and attempts to make an Indo-British commercial treaty before the transfer of power, it becomes clear that in spite of its debtor status the West was still dictating India's financial and economic conditions.

Britain's India trade for the period of time following independence has been estimated at a volume of two billion *Pound Sterling*. The question was raised whether there should be a '*trade treaty before final transfer of power*' in order to secure the volume of trade by treaty and to grant the British priority in trading with India.

In this way Indian imports of consumer goods would have been a means of decreasing Great Britain's *sterling debts*. The threat of inflation could have been 'warded off' by the imports. Unfortunately, the British export business did not have sufficient capacities to satisfy the demand in India.

The *American world trade proposals* were another barrier. In this matter, Indians and Americans were of the same opinion. Both felt that an open world trading system would allow India to engage in free trade regardless of the imperial preferences or other special agreements. In order to finance this new way of trading, India wanted to make use of its accumulated sterling assets in London, as well as its assets in the USA. India's view on the availability of sterling assets was not entirely correct. Although a portion of the *Sterling Balances* were available for unrestricted use, as had been set down in the agreement with Great Britain, trading on the basis of sterling assets was only possible in the *Sterling Area*. Convertibility was a component of Britain's agreement with the United States. Nevertheless, Great Britain considered the stability of the *Pound Sterling* to be endangered, were it to allow the unlimited convertibility of the accumulated sterling assets.

The Indian government was also one of the parties involved in the economic rebuilding of India. Liesching spoke out in favour of contact between Indians and the British as quickly as possible to formalise the registry of Indian wishes for investment goods. Demand was high because during the war import controls prevented investment goods from being imported, and therefore there was a lot of catching up to do. Statistics for industrial production in British-India for the year 1946 reflect distribution in the provinces and in the sectors of industry. These include export and import data on Indian trade with Great Britain, Indian imports of British machinery, an investment prognosis, investors in India and information about rupee guarantees by the Indian government.

On 28 February 1947, after elections in the Indian provinces, the first 'Indian' budget was introduced into the central parliament in New Delhi. It was criticised by the Indian National Congress and the Indian principalities. Tax policies of the Minister of Finance met with especially sharp criticism. The speech given by the minister on the budget was an indication of how dependent the Indians still were on Great Britain. The speech, however, could also be taken as a mosaic of the approaching independence. It offers evidence that economic relations between Great Britain and India were still characterised by the political supremacy of the British, but that they were also slowly falling apart. In the subsequent parliamentary debate, Nehru criticised the roll of the British General Governor in the transition period, his semi-dictatorial authorities in economic policies, his powers to decide over import and export controls. The import control policy of the Indian government was criticised as being to slow and inefficient. The strictness practised in currency control made it difficult for businesses to import capital and other goods from outside the *Sterling Area* system. Nehru demanded that as many goods as possible be deleted from the *list of controlled items* and placed on the *open general licence for the Sterling Area*. Goods necessary for daily life were permitted to be imported as long as they did not effect the stability of the national economy and did not diminish currency reserves. Importing from outside the sterling block was only allowed if the products could be obtained comparatively cheaper and quicker than from inside the block. A further change in import restrictions was criticised: *"further the burden of providing non-availability has been shifted to Government from the importer so that it is now for the Government to satisfy themselves by their own enquiries whether goods required to be imported from outside the sterling area are available within it or not, instead of, as heretofore, asking the importer to prove that they were not so available."*

Criticism was also directed against further increases in the *Sterling Balances* at the *Bank of England* in London. The balance of *Account I* rose in the period between 2 September 1945 and 1 March 1946 by over Rs. 209 Crores. Less that a fifth of this amount could be attributed to the *Financial Settlement*.

Further criticised was the practice of the British government to continue importing aid from India on a credit basis. Special laws made this possible during the war, but this was no longer in the interest of the Indian economy after the war.

This was a possibility for the British government after Indian independence to set up an indirect rule over India by way of financial and economic hegemony. Articles 40 and 41 of the *Reserve Bank of India Act* were the legal foundation for 'acquiring' sterling assets during the war. These articles were never questioned while they were being used by the British government to justify unlimited disposal, as was shown in the previous chapter. It would not have been possible to repeal the *Act* at this time without creating chaos in British financial markets, at a time when Britain was trying to balance its payments and international credit institutions were being set up.

Nonetheless, how would it have been possible for the British government to have paid for imports except by following existing practice?

Another proposal aimed for taking on a short-term loan programme of the British government on a rupee basis. Enquiries on 1 April 1946 showed the possibility of improving Indo-British relations, especially if the British government understood these as meaning that the accumulated sterling assets could be taken into consideration.

What trade demand the British government would support in India and how much the current exports from India to Great Britain cost were still unclear. A calculation of current demands was made by the Indian government's Ministry of Finance:

- India should withdraw from the *Empire-Dollar-Pool*
- India should be given back dollars gained during the war from the pool

- India should receive gold or foreign currency for export surpluses
- India should withdraw from the pool if Britain's balance of trade with hard-currency countries should become unfavourable
  or if British net payments were available in proportion to total currency reserves of the *Sterling Area*
  or if the Anglo-American loan agreement should be ratified.

The financial question received a discreet touch by way of Article Seven of the Anglo-American agreement. Negotiations over the *Sterling Balances* and the Anglo-American agreement led the *Reserve Bank of India* to the following resolution:

"Left to sterling balances negotiations, but in view of delay that is taking place in ratification of Anglo-American loan, the uncertainty as to the time when the negotiations can be held and the insistent demand for some immediate action to prevent a further accumulation of sterling balances, we feel an interim arrangement should be made." An interim solution was seen as contributing to the possibility of political stability in India:

"To prevent further accrual of sterling in the manner in which it has hitherto accrual and to make free foreign exchange more readily available for Indian needs. It would have the greatest possible political advantage."

In order to better get a better picture of the economic situation in India and in anticipation of Indian independence and of the approaching negotiations over the *Sterling Balances*, the Indian government's Finance Ministry made a prognosis of the Indian trade balance and balance of payments for the year 1947.

The decrease in shipping tonnage to India as a consequence of import restrictions was balanced out during the first nine months of 1947 by the importing of high-quality goods. In this manner, from total imports worth £17 million, India received £4.9 million worth of textile machines from Great Britain .

The increase in American imports at the beginning of 1947 was dramatic. Among these were refrigerators, cars and trucks.

In the meantime, the India Office thought about aiming for a reduction of the sterling assets during 1948. It worked out a plan for estimating the Indian balance of payments for the period of time between 1947 and 1952. Estimating an independent India's balance of payments was part of the strategy prepared for the negotiations of the *Sterling Balances*. The goal was to maintain the frozen assets in London. The British government needed these assets as security for its debts to the United States.

These estimates of India's balance of payments were based on calculations made by the British Treasury. The India Office set its calculations to the *Bank of*

England, where they could be corrected with estimates made there. The India Office was in possession of a detailed listing of estimated balances of payments for India.

These estimates of Indian balance of payments for the period of time between 1947 and 1952 were completed before the Viceroy's proclamation in India on 3 June 1947. The coming constitutional changes in India were set down in the so-called *3 June Plan*. At first glance, the economic and financial policies of India were not affected.

Existing import control measures were expanded onto both of the new dominions. Imports of important goods such as wheat, legumes and flour came at the expense of the future Indian Dominion.

India's balance of payments for the year 1947 was as follows:

Exports: Rs 378.91 Crores

Imports: Rs. 363.00 Crores

India's balance of payments surplus: Rs. 15.91 Crores

For exports the following basis of calculation was used: Most of the goods were exported under the export restrictions of the Indian government. Most of these goods were subject to price controls.

For imports, these were subject to the condition that the Indian government have access to the *Sterling Balances* and free disposal of the *Empire-Dollar-Pool*.

Having statistics over the flow of goods strengthened the position of the British in negotiating over the *Sterling Balances*. The British delegation was informed about India's stability, economic framework and foreign trade. The statistics reflected the value of exports from India to selected hard-currency countries such as the United States, Canada, the Philippines, Argentina and Switzerland. The first three places belonged to the USA, Canada and Switzerland. The United States received by far the largest amount of Indian export goods. For this reason, India was in possession of large dollar reserves that held up the *Sterling System*.

After this discussion of economic and financial policies, there follows a discussion of another type, a discussion of the British lobby for India.

6.1. British Economic Interests in India Lobbying and *Safeguarding*

Lobbying

As the Indo-British negotiations over a financial settlement of the *Sterling Balances* drew near, British business was aspiring to safeguard and secure its interests in colonial and independent India. The chances of success were dimmed at the start. Both the Secretary of State for India and the Prime Minister excluded these ambitions in their official proclamations. Attlee, the British Prime Minister, made a historical proclamation before the British parliament on 20 February 1947. He announced the withdrawal of the British from India by June 1948 at the latest and the transfer of power to the potential rulers in Delhi, but failed to mention in any way the future position of British business in an independent India.

What kind of business interests did the British have in India, what were their goals, how did they hope to influence British policies in order to achieve their aims?

British interests in India were safeguarded by various groups and agencies. Numerous organisations represented 'European' interests in India.

Central Constitutional Committee
Chambers of Commerce
European Association
Indo-Burma Association

These agencies offered protection, even legal protection for British business interests in India. These groups meant trouble for the closing of a commercial agreement between Great Britain and the successor nations of British-India and the Indian principalities. The British representation in India was uncompromising in its pressure on the British government in London. Nonetheless, the pressure group of British business, the *Joint Committee on India* , was not able to prevail against the political constellations in India and the British government in London. Why not?

The British government would not consider taking part in negotiations over such a pact with representatives of the Indian independence movement at the time of the *transfer of power*. In the same way, it refused to negotiate over a protectionist amendment to help secure the position of British business. The inner stability of India rested on shaky foundations and did not allow the British government any other option.

The British side had other difficulties to contend with. The British business lobby in India had to gain the impression that the British government was standing up for its interests in India and also representing these interests during the negotiations over the *transfer of power*.

The only reference to British business interests was to be found in Paragraph 14 of Attlees proclamation in February 1947:

"(The) Government will consider all aspects of the problem of sterling balances with a view to arriving at the most beneficial and equitable settlement."

How could British business interests in India be achieved? After the barrier of commercial guarantees was removed, and trade licences were granted to an Indian partner, there arose the question of investment possibilities.

What kind of picture was there for importing capital in India in 1947?

The necessity of this *registration scheme* was to be seen in the large number of goods required for Indian industry, as foreseen in Article 2 of the *India (central government) Legislature Act, 1946*. This regulation remained until 1 April 1947 in power. It secured control over currency holdings. In this way, the Indian government tried to attain balanced trading and a favourable foreign trade balance.

British business interest was not confined to the territory of British-India. The terms on which British-India stood with the Indian principalities should be considered in light of the approaching independence and of the resources and economic capacities of the principalities. Also to be considered: the chance for British business, making use of a settlement worked out by the British government, to deal before independence with fewer politically and economically responsible parties.

THE CENTRAL INDIAN GOVERNMENT AND THE PRINCIPALITIES

The Indian government's industrial policy was aimed to co-ordinate the industrial policies of the provinces and the principalities. The central Indian government in Delhi had trouble co-ordinating the economic initiatives and economic plans of the provinces, and putting, for the most part, a stop to economic secessionist tendencies. It needed to maintain its influence and preserve the political and economic unity of the country during the phase of political *transfer of power* to the Indians. Informative in this light is a letter by Lord Pethick-Lawrence to the Viceroy, Lord Wavell. Pethick-Lawrence described the difficulties the central Indian government had with the government of Hyderabad. These had to do partly with the importing of investment goods and smaller manufacturing systems to Hyderabad. As the *transfer of power* approached, it was desirable from the minister's point of view not to provoke a confrontation between the governments in Delhi and Hyderabad. At the time, however, the constitutional fundamentals left it uncertain as to how and with which means Hyderabad could have been prevented from importing investment goods and machinery. The Secretary of State for India condemned steps taken by the Ministry of Trade in Delhi to stop Hyderabad's imports simply because these did not fit into Delhi's overall economic policy.

The national independence movement wanted to achieve a linking of the economic centralisation with the political centralisation of India. Nehru did not want to see the 'Balkanisation' of India. The political and economic goal of the first independent Indian government was a unified economic territory.

This was also the goal of the central Indian government before independence. For British economic relations with the principalities, there were the same terms as with British-India.

To co-ordinate British economic relations with the principalities, Great Britain set up the post of a British *Industrial Commissioner* in India. His task was to establish new contacts between individual industrialists and British firms, and to cultivate existing ones.

By commission of the British government, he worked out plans, as allowed by his competencies, for the industrial development of India. These plans included *joint ventures* of British industrialists during the *transition period.*

Great Britain and the Indian Principalities

Trade between India and Great Britain was of a special nature as the independence of India approached.

The India Office wanted to know how the principalities were to be handled under international law after 15 August 1947. This included how to handle them in the economic sphere. Were they to continue to profit from the imperial preferences granted by Britain to its colonies? Or were they under international law to be considered sovereign states and thus placed economically on the same level as the USA and the rest of Great Britain's partners in trade? What was to be the foundation for carrying on trade within all of India?

The different fractions at the India Office in London reached a compromise, to arrange a so-called *Standstill Agreement.* Substance of this agreement was as follows: the Indo-British trade agreement of 1931 would be retained until a new agreement took affect between Great Britain and India on the one hand, and between India and the principalities on the other; until then the principalities would not be part of the Indian union.

The pressure of the British government on the Indian government and the Indian delegation at the international World Trade Conference in Geneva took effect. A letter on 12 August 1947 from Robert Burns to P. Harris of the *Commonwealth Relations Trade Department* shows that Great Britain was forced to act under American pressure.

The Secretary of State for India, Earl of Listowel, commented on the difficulties of the *Standstill Agreement* in an international context.

"The Effect of clause 7(i)(b) of Indian Independence Bill will be to raise question of application to states of Indo-U.K. trade agreement of 1939. It would however be administratively extremly difficult to treat goods from Indian states differently from goods from India on entry into U.K. and still more difficult to distinguish between goods from different Indian states. Consequently our provisional view, which we shall confirm, is that we should continue to give states goods benefit of British preferential tariff until long term position of States is clarified so long as states do not alter the existing arrangements so far as they are concerned. We believe that we are reasonably covered under U.K. legislation by section 2(i) of Ottawa Agreements Acts 1932 read with Section 21 of Import Duties Act, 1942. But in any case legality of our action under U.K. law is unlikely to be challenged."

A number of foreign powers complained about Britain's practice of granting the Indian principalities customs preferences. The British government countered by referring to the trade policy practice of the United States. The USA was granting the Philippines, newly independent, trade advantages. At the same time, the United States, by way of the Anglo-American Loan Agreement of December 1945 and Article Seven of the *Lend-Lease Act*, was pressing Great Britain to lift and repeal British preference duties and preferred treatment of British imports from the colonies.

The policy of *Standstill Agreements* with the Indian principalities was the British government's declared goal, both during negotiations with the Indian independence movement and during debates in the British lower house of Parliament.

One of the topics for the international World Trade Conference was this link between the granting of imperial preferences and India's status under international law and also the Indian principalities after 15 August 1947. The constitutional development in India was affected by Article 14 of the *ITO Charter* and Article 1(2) of the conference's *General Agreement*. Despite Article 14 of the charter, *National Autonomy*, the British side was convinced that there were no difficulties to be seen in the further granting of imperial preferences to India and to other dominions, even if India were to leave the Commonwealth.

Was it possible to grant *imperial preference* to an independent India as to other foreign countries?

Bilateral trade agreements secured Great Britain currency revenues. In order to prevent misinterpretations, the British delegation at the International World Trade Conference proposed adding a note in *Appendix A* of the charter with reference to *Article 14 (2) (A)(II)* and with the wording *"as on April 10, 1947"*. The addition was easily defended, as India was in the process of constitutional change. The constitutional negotiations were freed of the question of granting imperial preferences to India and to the Indian principalities. However, should the two strands be joined - constitutional negotiations with the Indian side and negotiations of Indo-British economic relations - then there would be the danger of existing agreements being annulled legally.

There was still a danger that could not be ignored if British-India were divided under international law after independence, a danger that would affect Indo-British economic relations. Would the Indian principalities profit from the still-valid British practice of customs preferences and thus make themselves an economically better trading position with third countries in the Asian region? The danger was not unfounded, as the Indian principalities were considered internationally as part of the British Empire. The British government stuck to this status for the time after 15 August 1947. The British government cemented this status with a so-called *Standstill Agreement* in order to reach *"continued fulfilment of the existing international engagements applicable to the Indian States."*

An agreement between the Indian principalities and the two independent dominions of India and Pakistan established economic and financial continuity. The Indian principalities and the governments of the two independent dominions of India and Pakistan agreed provisionally to an organic type of co-operation until constitutional assemblies in all states involved could meet and decide over further proceedings.

Safeguarding

Financial safeguards are to be distinguished from the *safeguards* of the British business lobby. The *financial safeguards* were in connection with the founding of the Reserve Bank of India in 1934. At that time, constitutional concessions were worked out and granted to the Indians by the British government in the *Government of India Act, 1935*. Among other things, these were financial autonomy for the Indian provinces and an codifying of the division of powers between various administrative institutions. With the establishment of the Reserve Bank of India, the British prevented the Indian Minister of Finance in a future Indian transitional government from deciding on monetary policy. This area of financial autonomy granted to the Indians was placed within the competencies of the Reserve Bank of India, which was modelled on the Bank of England and had the nature of a private institution.

In addition, there were the constitutional guarantees, *Safeguards section 111-121* of the *Government of India Act, 1935*. These consolidated the position of British business in India. On the basis of these legally anchored guarantees, British firms founded subsidiaries in India with *limited* status. In this way they were on an equal footing with Indian companies and circumvented the high hurdles of Indian protectionist duties. These hurdles had been set up to stabilise Indian industry, but British companies were now able to utilise this protection, avoid the *Capital Goods Registration Scheme* and compete in the post-war period.

On 4 December 1945, the chairman of the *All-India Manufacturers' Organization* wrote an urgent appeal to the Secretary of State for India to abolish the constitutional guarantees of British business in India. This would be absolutely necessary if he wanted to solve the political problems of India. This controversy had been going on since the *Cripps Mission* in 1942.

This was the Indian point of view. The British one was, of course, different. British business promised India to deliver, within the export capacities of Britain, the goods required to build up the Indian economy. British export businesses expected the Indian industry to maintain closer contact with the British export business. In view of India's strong position on the basis of the Indian sterling assets in London, the British export business was very interested in orders from India; this would mean that Britain could eliminate its trade deficit with India and pay off its credit to the United States. Nehru considered the *safeguards* of British business an obstacle. The Indian government had already promised to revoke the guarantees for the British export business at the end of the war in 1945, but the government still refused to this, despite American intervention. Concerning the interests of the British export business, Mr. Turnbull at the Indian Office wrote to Sir William Croft on 14 March 1946 that the British Minister of Trade had placed British economic interests in India at disposal. He advised not to make the British export business any overly clear promises about a trade agreement with India. An increase in efforts by British exporters would help reduce British *sterling debts* in India over the long run.

The struggle over the guarantees for British business – Articles 111 to 121 of the Indian constitution of 1935 – was coming to a head. The minister in the Indian government responsible for the planning of Indian industrial development during the transfer of power phase was Sir Ardeshir Dalal. For building up the Indian economy, he compiled a list of items reaching from farm machinery to cement machines.

In its first letter of 27 March 1945, the *All-India Manufacturers' Organisation* had notified the Secretary of State for India in London that Sir Dalal had failed in his attempt to speak with representatives of the British export business about the *Safeguarding Sections* in the 1935 constitution. These complicated the carrying out of the economic programme for the Indian government. Dalal had a decisively negative view of the Safeguard sections in the constitution Act. The existing privileges were disturbing the relationship of the Indian government to British business in India as these safeguards were linked to the economic hegemony of British business interests in India. Dalal appealed to the British government to abolish the privileges by vote of parliament. This reflected the trust of Indians that the British government was seriously interested in solving constitutional problems in India.

This was another indication of the interlinking of politico-constitutional problems with economic pressures that resulted from the constitutional realities of the *Government of India Act, Articles 111 to 121*.

6.2. British Business and Negotiations over the Indo-British Commercial Agreement on the Eve of the *Transfer of Power*

In the period before the passing of the *Indian Independence Act, 1947* the interest of British business in India became politically virulent. After the proclamation of 3 June 1947, the Secretary of State for India suggested a hearing of the *Joint Committee on India* to insure a co-ordination of the government's policies with the interests of British business. The committee's chairman was afraid that during the transitional period until an independent Indian government was established, British business would be without any legal protection in India. Sir Carr asked for an interim solution to restore the confidence of British business in India and ensure that business be continued under the existing circumstances. A new commercial agreement had to follow at the latest after the establishment of a new Indian government. Under the existing political circumstances, no detailed working out of a new agreement was envisioned. The committee was afraid that the safeguards of the 1935 constitution would be repealed by the Indian parliament after independence, as these were seen as an obstacle in the economic development of India.

Of what nature was the interim agreement supposed to be?

The British Minister of Trade proposed that the interests of British business could be 'voluntarily' transferred into the new agreement analogous to the safeguard articles of the 1935 constitution. But the *Joint Committee on India* was afraid that this solution might be rejected. For this reason the British Minister of Trade suggested working out an interim agreement analogous to the treaties between Great Britain and the dominions. However, these 'treaties' were based on verbal agreements. This was in accordance with English *Common Law* constitutional tradition. It was advantageous for the British to avoid exact definitions or attempts at exact agreements, because of the danger of misinterpretations, misinterpretations that might block an interim commercial agreement. The British Minister of Trade initiated a round of negotiations in India after the elections in the Indian provinces had brought forth an undisputed Indian negotiating partner. Nonetheless, a new commercial agreement was only to be signed in politically more peaceful times. Negotiations over the *Sterling Balances* were being carried on at the same time, and negative results in these would have had negative effects on any new commercial agreement. In this matter the Secretary of State for India agreed with the Minister of Trade. A failure of the sterling negotiations would have detrimental effects on the position of British business in India.

As to when negotiations with the Indians over a Indo-British commercial agreement could begin, this depended on the formulation of economic policies by British-India's successor nations, Pakistan and India. Without an economic plan, an investment framework, especially in India, it was not possible to begin negotiations. Existing currency regulations stipulated that company proceeds could only be transferred to foreign countries after paying for investments in India. The closer definition of the type of investment was a major barrier to possible negotiations. This was also the context for reducing the *Sterling Balances* debts. If good results could be achieved from the *Sterling Balances* negotiations, then the British government could assume a greater readiness to invest on the part of British business and a greater willingness to co-operate on the part of the Indians. To members of the delegation from the British Treasury to the *Sterling Balances* negotiations, Patel promised a pro-British atmosphere for

Indo-British economic co-operation, if satisfactory results could be achieved by July 1947. Everything began to focus on July 1947 as the culmination point:

- The Anglo-American loan agreement obliged Great Britain to make the *Pound Sterling* convertible by July 1947.
- Settlement of British *sterling debts* in India was to be reached by July 1947.
- A new legal framework for British investments was created by the Indian government in July 1947.

On 10 July 1947, the British Prime Minister Clement Attlee commented on a Indo-British commercial agreement during the second reading of the *Indian Independence Bill*:

"It has, therefore, not been possible to negotiate agreements with the successor authorities, though it is our intention to begin such negotiations when the new Indian Government are in the saddle. Apart from matters arising out of the transfer of power, there are other important matters on which we hope to have negotiations with the Indian and Pakistan Governments. We desire to establish, by free negotiations, close, cordial and effective arrangements with both new Dominions in all fields affecting our common interests, and particularly in regard to defence matters and in the economic field."

The prime minister's comments were reflected by Great Britain's interim agreements with Pakistan and India after independence. The *Indian Independence Act, 1947 Section 9(1)(c)* and the *India (provisional constitution) order, 1947* and the *Pakistan (Provisional constitution) order, 1947* abolished the discriminating *Safeguardings* of the *Government of India Act, 1935 Art. 111 to 121*. British business, however, feared disadvantages in remaining in the successor nations of British-India after 15 August 1947 without the constitutional safeguards. The *Joint Committee on India* took a different position to that of the India Office and the British government.

Despite the widespread fears of British business in India, the British government reacted calmly to the demands of British-Indian business lobbyists.

The fears of legal insecurity on the part of British business remained, especially fears of Indian discrimination and of losing good position in the Indian market.

As the transfer of power to India approached, the India Office wrote a memorandum concerning a possible commercial agreement with India. It outlined the urgency of British business interests in India, indicated limits and volumes of trade in the agreement, and referred to a later point of time for taking up negotiations on an agrement, up to two years at the latest after the *transfer of power*. The danger of British business losing legal protection in India was recognised, and the securing of provisional agreement envisioned. The India Office placed two conditions for working out an agreement:

1. Negotiations for making a commercial agreement were to be taken up two years at the latest after the *transfer of power* to India.
2. Until negotiations were taken up, the provisional agreement remained binding. It could be cancelled by either side at six months' notice. This clause was to become effective only 27 months after the *transfer of power* and was to end automatically three months before taking up negotiations over a permanent commercial agreement.

In May 1947, the India Office developed offers for a provisional commercial agreement that was to be worked out while negotiations over the *transfer of power* were being held. The 'Indianisation' – participation of Indians in key positions – was speeded up. A quota for capital participation was set at 30%. The Indian government secured raw materials for the British utilities business and worked out a distribution scheme for the British export business. In the event that India should leave the *Commonwealth*, the question of India's economic and political status had to be solved.

The solution was complicated by the fact that the United States had offered India a trade agreement in January 1947. The *India and Burma Committee* was concerned about the rise of the USA as competing trade partner in South Asia. With the Anglo-American *Financial Agreement* of December 1945, the United States secured its economic and political supremacy in South Asia.

In working out a commercial treaty, the British Board of Trade was undecided as to the type of agreement. *What form of interim agreement?* The Board of Trade decided that *"it would be advantageous to avoid any precise definition or any attempt to get precise agreement on individual points."* The Board knew as well that *"sterling balances and commercial relationship might well affect each other."* The legal framework and the drafting of the new commercial treaty were to be made in such a way that it would be possible *"to see a satisfactory commercial treaty covering british business men's rights in the new India."*

In his memorandum the Secretary of State for India recommended separate negotiations leading to a commercial treaty and to a constitutional *transfer of power* agreement. The separation of political *transfer of power* from a commercial agreement was to be ruled out. The minister felt that Great Britain's financial weakness was to be seen as the origin of concessions made to India's drive for independence, to the *Congress* and to the *Moslem League*. On 30 July

1942, the parliamentary under-secretary at the India Office, the Duke of Devonshire, had drawn attention to these circumstances in the British upper house, saying:

"His Majesty's Government made it clear when they made, through the Lord Privy Seal, their recent effort to arrive at a solution of India's constitutional problems, that a guarantee of special protection for british commercial interests in India would not be a condition for the acceptance of whatever constitution Indians might evolve after the war and that such provisions would properly be a matter for negotiation with the future Government of India."

The memorandum closed with the comment that Britain's long political and economic connection with India were not to leave British business interests in India unprotected. In the event that an Indo-British interim solution should fail in the sector of bilateral trade, the British government would be subjected to intense criticism in the British parliament. The India Office reported to the British *High Commissioner* in India that there was a growing readiness on the part of Indian industry to work together with the British. Both the India Office and the Board of Trade saw this as an opportunity for India's economic development in the period after independence.

"India was faced with major problems of economic adjustments at the same time that partition plus independence had presented her with a political problem in some ways unexampled."

British economic interests in India collided with those of the United States in the period before independence. Economic and financial weaknesses meant that Great Britain could not keep India tied to its former colonial master in the post-war period, as India had grown politically and financially stronger. Attempts to tie India after independence per commercial treaty to Great Britain were thwarted by its competitor on the Indian subcontinent and in the Southeast Asia, the United States.

6.3. Negotiations over the Sterling Balances 1947

The wartime economy and foreign credit necessitated by the war weakened Britain's position with the allied nations, most especially with the USA. Britain's foreign debts, also to members of the British Empire, contributed to this position after the war. Settling Britain's *sterling debts* became the focus of attention in relations between Great Britain and India during the post-war period. To finance its economic development, India disposed over sterling assets in London. London 'held' these assets but was, at the same time, in debt to the United States and to other Empire countries. How were these conflicts of interest to be solved. What would a solution look like? Negotiations over the *Sterling Balances* did not affect Indo-British relations alone. The part played be the United States added a third component to the bilateral character of the negotiations, extending it to a triangular relationship.

Why did these negotiations take on such an immense importance in Indo-British economic relations before India's independence? What was linked to the results of these negotiations? Which economic and financial consequences did these talks and their actual results have for Great Britain and for an India soon to be independent?

The *Sterling Balances* are the pivoting point in Indo-British economic relations before and after India's independence. Before independence it was the accumulation of British sterling war debts in London. This involved the British wartime economy and detailed British economic plans for the post-war period. After independence it was the elimination of Britain's awkward wartime *sterling debts*. Decisive in this were the new post-war role for Great Britain in the circle of economic powers, and Britain's dependency on the economic superpower USA before and after the war. Great Britain missed its chance to compensate for the loss of its empire by entering into the process of European integration in the 1950s.

The problem area mentioned here will be approached in three steps. In the first step, India's position during and after the war will be presented. In the second step, the views of the British business lobby will be discussed. In the context of working out strategies for negotiations over a new Indo-British commercial treaty, this lobby had already made an attempt to influence the British government. In the third and final step, the negotiations between Great Britain and India will be described. The present work will expand the here-to-fore limited view of Indo-British relations by adding a third component to it and expanding it to a triangular relationship.

6.3.1. British-India's Position

From September 1939 to March 1946, India accumulated Rs. 405 Crores worth of US dollars in the *Empire Dollarpool* and spent Rs. 240 Crores. India had a surplus of Rs. 165 Crores. India's payments into the pool in 1945/46 reached, since it had to make payments to Canada, Sweden, Switzerland and

Portugal, a total of about Rs. 124 Crores. Until the end of the second quarter of 1946, India withdrew larger sums to finance the importing of food imports and other goods.

India's three most important trading partners were Great Britain , the United States and the Empire countries.

The United States was interested in exhausting India's export capacities, despite the *Atlantic Charter* and *Article Seven* of the *Reciprocal Aid Agreement* of February 1942.

Fact was, however, that India would remain dependent on the *Empire Market*. 61% of its total exports in 1940/41 went to Empire countries. In 1938 it had transacted only 54% of its trading with the Empire. Viewing India's dependency from the perspective of its sterling creditors, its dependency would only seem greater if the following were assumed: an increase in demand in Britain's own domestic market and a political trend to international free trade. These deliberations were only conceivable in Gregory's scenario during the war. Reality after the war was quite different.

Political conditions in India were also important for the sterling negotiations. India desperately needed goods and services to provide for the population and to realise its economic plans:

1. imports of consumer goods
2. imports of food and raw materials
3. imports of industrial goods and investment goods –
   machinery works, factory technology, technical support, etc.

The wartime transformation of industrial production had the effect that certain products did not have to be imported any longer during the war, for example, pharmaceutical products, petrochemical products and electrical equipment.

On the other hand, imports of consumer goods rose to support the Indian population. The negotiations over the *Sterling Balances* had become necessary to avert a cabinet crisis of the British-Indian government. The negotiations could not be avoided since with the ending of the war the function of capitalising the war was fulfilled.

But what was, in fact, India's position at the time?

BRITISH-INDIA'S BALANCE OF PAYMENTS

During the course of World War Two, India moved from debtor to creditor. India's balance of trade changed to the advantage of India. More exports than imports, a result of export and import controls, led to an elimination and amortisation of interest and pre-war debts by 1942. Pension payments, salaries of

British officers in India, transfer of profits for foreign investments in India and payments of bank, shipping and insurance fees contributed to this. The trade surplus and the positive balance of payments with Great Britain were used to finance Indian railways and to repatriate Indian *sterling debts* of the pre-war period. British wartime debts for Indian war goods were accounted for in the form of frozen assets, the *Sterling Balances*, in the *Bank of England.*

In the first few years after the war India produced a deficit in its balance of payments. This trend was continued in the years that followed. Reason for this was the rise in demand for consumer goods. Another reason was the necessity to import food essential in overcoming supply bottlenecks.

6.3.2. Viewpoint of British Business Lobby and British Politics

British business circles directly affected by trade with India were following the development of the sterling assets negotiations between the British and the Indian governments very attentively. British business hoped for a 'good settlement' for all parties in the negotiations. This meant that they would be able to convert the economy from wartime to peacetime production and manage the 'transfer of power' from British to Indian hands. If it were simply for the British side to decide about the sterling assets, then there would be no problem finding an acceptable solution - this was the British point of view. However, the effects of other factors could not be calculated. The British deficit, the weak economy after the war and rising prices on the basis of the dollar were only some of the factors that were responsible for the poor results of the American loans. The Minister of State at the India Office took the following standpoint on the negotiations over *Sterling Balances*:

"There is one point in connection with the current political developments to which Economic Department cannot but attach importance. This is the relation between the Secretary of State and the British Business Community as represented by the Joint Committee on India. These relations in London and also in India have hitherto been reasonably cordial and a useful measure of confidence has, we think, been built up in the minds of the business representatives. If nothing is said to them in the very near future, our view is that these relations may become severely strained - in the light of the tone of the meeting of 13 May, the Joint Committee might even be able to make out a case that understandings then reached had been broken - the business interests would put the dogs on as soon as a debate occurs in Parliament and their co-operation

in the future might be given less heartedly. It is not suggested that they should be given any details of what exactly H.M.G. propose as we understand this is still highly secret. We think however, that a gesture of politeness should be made either orally or perhaps better by means of a short letter to the Secretary of Committee."

In negotiating with India over the *financial settlement*, the British expected that abandoning the *safeguarding clauses* of the *Government of India Act, 1935* would mean disadvantages for the British export business. What was the official Indian policy in the *Sterling Balances* question? Officially, the Indian government was in favour of giving the accumulated sterling assets as sureties to the Reserve Bank of India. This would mean having larger currency reserves and more working capital in the bank business. These assets could then be used by the government to buy British goods in India. Secondly, the *Sterling Balances* could be set up as a fund. In this respect the Indian Minister of Finance made the following statement with the approval of the Secretary of State for India:

"Government will consider all aspects of the problem of sterling balances with view to arriving at the most beneficial and equitable settlement." In commenting, the Secretary of State for India touched on the importance of Indo-British economic relations. This importance was, among other things, a question of the quality of relations between the parties to the agreement. The British would not grant protection to any agreement unless it was based on mutual*goodwill*.

In this respect the British government had to work on convincing British business about India; the author saw quite clearly that *"only adequate treaty protection can assure their position"*. For this reason Britain made every possible effort to work about a permanent commercial treaty with India after independence. Since 1942 it had been clear to the British government that the *transfer of power* to Indians was inevitable, irrespective of whether any commercial treaty or economic agreement were to be signed. While Britain and India were trying to work out a provisional commercial treaty, the sterling assets were diminishing. After reaching an all-time high of £1.3 billion in 1946, they were down to £1.2 billion on 31 January 1947. As the Indian Minister of Finance explained,

"The sterling balances represent, by and large, the entire reserve of foreign exchange which this country will have at its disposal in the years to come for purchases of capital equipment required for our development programme and for meeting any unfavourable balance of payments. It is, therefore, a matter of paramount importance for our future to see that, apart from those consumer goods of which our people are badly and urgently in need, these balances should be wisely spent in the purchase of capital goods and the creation of

productive assets, and should not be allowed to be frittered away, for instance on luxuries, trifles or non-essential consumer goods in a manner which does not add to the real wealth of the country. To ensure wise spending abroad is a responsibility of Government of India and I can assure the House that they are alive to this responsibility."

The importance of the immanent constitutional changes made it extremely urgent to find a solution to the *sterling debts* question. In an address to the Indian central parliament, the Indian Minister of Finance explained that the Indian accumulated sterling assets in London were a result of India's voluntary support of the war burden for Britain and the Allies. This can certainly be questioned. The Minister of Finance assured the Indian parliament that he would do his best to achieve a fair settling of British debts. He had nothing to say, however, about how he wanted to do this.

6.3.3. Indo-British Negotiations

After outlining the position of British-India, the views of the British business lobby and the policies of the British government, the following section will be devoted to the negotiations themselves.

'Talks on sterling balances to begin' was the headline to a report on the negotiations over the *Sterling Balances* in the 4 January 1947 issue of *Commerce*. The British delegation had the task of averting an impending cabinet crisis of the Indian transitional government and working out an agreement acceptable to all sides. Cabinet members from the Indian Congress Party threatened to resign if concrete results were not achieved in this matter.

The British delegation was led by Sir Wilfrid Eady, representative of the British Treasury. Other delegates were:

Mr. P.S. Beale from the *Bank of England.*

Mr. C.F. Cobbold, deputy governor of the *Bank of England.*

Mr. Anderson from the India Office

Mr. J. Nasmyth from the British Treasury.

All five delegates to the negotiations were considered professionals in financial matters and hard-boiled diplomats. Points to be negotiated were:

1. Great Britain's position in international affairs after the war.
2. The unbearable burden of the wartime *sterling debts* for Britain.
3. India's inflexible position in the issue of making concessions.
4. The British government's position in questions of interest on loans.

Three items were set on the agenda for negotiations:
1. The problem of the *Sterling Balances* for Great Britain
2. Information required on the *Sterling Balances*
3. Sources of this information.

The first item took in the *Pound Sterling* as an international means of payment, the importance of the problem and Great Britain's possibilities for paying off these debts. For the third item, information on export capacities and imports needed for the years 1947 to 1952 were required.

The problem of the *Sterling Balances* was linked to Indian trade policies. How many imports were foreseen from Great Britain, the *Sterling Area* and other counties? Which imports were foreseen for the realisation of the *Bombay Plan* and other economical development plans?

This context included imports of food, the Indian government's policy on precious metals, and ideas of the British government on how Indian import orders could be financed. What financial possibilities were there in the *Sterling Area*?

What possibilities did India have of financing these imports itself via Indian economic and export capacities?

Potentially there was the possibility of reducing the *sterling debts* in order to decrease the difference between Indian payments for imports and Indian ability to pay. Negotiations went on over the amount that Britain could possibly repay.

The strategy of the British side was aimed at the relationship between the *Balances* and the *Pound Sterling* as currency and at the structure of the bank business, the policies of the *Bank of England*. The British delegates sounded out possibilities and models for 'adjusting' the *Sterling Balances*. One of the amounts to be adjusted was India's disproportionate financial contribution to the Allied war effort. This contribution was counterbalanced by payments from the British budget for the British-Indian administration during the war. In addition, the British side at the negotiations referred to article 10(1)(c) of the Anglo-American loan agreement, which required a reduction of the *Sterling Balances*.

Another argument for reducing the amount of British *sterling debts* was the fact that the United States and Canada made payments to the benefit of India on the basis of *Lend-Lease*. These were *mutual aid*, credit and other compensation payments.

The British government pointed to similar agreements and negotiations with Egypt, Australia, New Zealand, Argentina, and other countries throughout the world.

The British negotiators proposed a debt reduction and the availability of funds for India to be able to finance imports needed. Responsibility for the control and realisation of the debt reduction was to be given to the *Bank of England*. Everything pointed in the direction of India waiving its rights.

Great Britain held out the prospect of lowering the amount Indian would have to disclaim in case the United States should disclaim British repayments demanded by the Anglo-American agreement of December 1945. The British legitimised their procedure to cancel debt repayment with the British potential to defend India during World War Two. Other points were releasing India from payment of British pensions for service during the colonial period and from any payments resulting from changes in the constitutional framework. A model for repaying the *Sterling Balances* was worked out by the *Bank of England*. An interest rate of one percent was placed on the Indian sterling assets, and India was enabled to dispose of these assets subject to prevailing rates of interest on credit. The two teams of negotiators agree to limit transfer of capital and investments 'by gentleman's agreement'.

There was little willingness on the part of the Indian negotiators to deal with the British proposal to unfreeze the sterling assets without interest. The negotiations were broken off after the Indian *Finance Member* Liaquat Ali Khan signalled that he was unwilling to compromise. Representatives of the Indian government should have been prepared for this, as the resignation of the Moslem Finance Minister was to be expected for political reasons. The Indian public expected some sort of concessions from the British. The Indian Finance Minister commented on the *Dollar Pool* and the *Sterling Balances*:

"India is still a member of the Sterling area. It follows therefore that it is still a member of the Empire Dollar Pool. I should like however to point out that there is, as far as India is concerned, a quantitative difference between the incidence of India's membership on the pool now, and her membership of that pool before the coming into force of the sterling balances Agreement of 14 August 1947."

Theoretically India could make unlimited withdrawals of currency from the *Empire-Dollar-Pool* that were urgently needed to finance the building of its economy. However, access to essential currencies was denied to India. After obtaining independence, India was not free of the policies of the *Bank of England* and of the British Treasury, not free to forge its own currency policy. The amount of money at India's disposal after independence was governed by the regulations that determined access to the sterling assets at the *Bank of England*, in the so called *Account No. 1*.

It goes without saying that the Indian sterling assets in London did not represent 'war-time profiteering', as Conservatives in the parliamentary opposition and business representatives in Great Britain maintained. On the contrary, these assets represented India's 'involuntary' readiness to share the burden of the war. The sterling assets did not result alone from deliveries of war goods, but also reflected in hard currency the existence of Indian invested capital that was entrusted to the *Bank of England*; these entrusted funds were mainly the result of gold and silver exports and private export trading. A committee of the British parliament had determined that the prices of Indian deliveries of aid were more favourable in comparison to those of other countries. For this reason, the British negotiators insisted that it would not be possible to account for India's extensive sterling assets in London solely with British transfer payments to India during the Second World War.

The British negotiators had been set to India to achieve results similar to those of the Anglo-American loan agreement. The Indian interim government rejected a lowering of the British *sterling debts* as foreseen in the Anglo-American loan agreement. The resulting room to manoeuvre in was very little. After six years of wartime economy, restrictions in consumer goods, negative foreign trade balance and negative balance of payments, Great Britain was factually in the position of a debtor. The British government expected concessions from its creditors. The former deputy governor of the Reserve Bank of India, Sir Manilal B. Nanavati, commented:

"Britain has never shown this kind of concession to India in the past. In spite of its poor economy, India was forced to carry for years a huge debt of over Rs. 400 crores at rates of interest which when viewed against present-day standard were ridiculously high and what is more important every pie of this debt was honoured without a murmur. Even on moral grounds U.K. has not such a strong case for demanding scaling down, especially because of the stepmotherly treatment that it meted out to India as compared with other members of the British Empire, during all the war years."

The former governor of the Reserve Bank of India commented further that all deliveries of aid to Australia, Canada and to South Africa that served the industrialisation of these countries, were made voluntarily. Notwithstanding, there were many barriers placed in the development of India's economy.

Repayment of British debts could not be achieved in a short term, but only over a period of 15 to 20 years' time. India needed this money, however, ad hoc for the building of its economy, e.g. for the financing of Indo-British co-operation.

6.4. Indo-British *Financial Settlement* of 1947

As a result of the negotiations over India's sterling assets in Great Britain, an agreement was made on 14 August 1947 between Great Britain and India, to leave India's accumulated sterling assets with few exceptions untouched until the end of 1947. One day before the *transfer of power*, the setting of India on an equal basis under international law with the rest of the nations of the world, the British and Indian governments signed an agreement that victimised the ambitious business plans of Indian industrials. From the first minute on as a sovereign nation in the area of financial policy, India was limited and financially strangled by this agreement. Not only that consumer goods had been restricted during the war and that export proceeds had been left as loans in the British mother country, India was expected to accept financial restrictions to the advantage of Great Britain, a country that was economically ruined for its own part. For this reason, Empire nations with sterling currency reserves accepted that all proceeds of trade with the United States on a dollar basis be transferred to London into a common fund. Furthermore, the *sterling* countries accepted the rule that only allowed themselves limited access to sterling currency assets in London. Decisive here was an interest in preventing the destabilisation of the British economy. The *sterling* countries could 'buy back' the currency hoarded in London via higher import quotas of British goods, as long as the British export business was in a position to fulfill such export quotas.The British also thought about a *Sterling Balances Blocking*, but how practicable was this?

In considering the elimination of debts, it was important to analyse economic tendencies in hard-currency countries, e.g., the development and strength of the US dollar after the war. The British government made every effort to achieve an agreement with the Indian government, also taking India's balance of payments for the year 1947 into consideration. India's deficit made it easier for the British to wrest concessions from the Indians in this matter.

The *Financial Agreement* of 14 August 1947

Justification for the Agreement from the British Viewpoint.

India had to be convinced of the necessity of the agreement. British concern in this matter was based on the economic difficulties of Britain after the war. The economically desolate situation after the war was covered up by *Lend-Lease* aid from the United States. In order to pay back existing *sterling debts* to creditor nations, it was necessary to raise production in Great Britain. Thus, it was both in the interests of Britain and of India to limit unnecessary British exports to India, that is, to limit India's access to its sterling assets in London as well. This reasoning, and the need for US currency as well, led the Indian government to issue import restrictions on goods from the United States and Great Britain, with exception of essential goods such as food and supplies for daily needs. A long-term solution to the problem was not in view. Internal political difficulties blocked the possibility of negotiations outside India, and India's interim government was not in a position to try to find a long-term solution. In July 1947, a small official delegation was carrying on negotiations in London and achieved results by the end of the month.

The agreement with India was oriented to the results of the British-Egyptian agreement.

Items one and two of the agreement summarise the use of and *Account No. 2*. For payment of outstanding accounts inside or outside the *sterling area*, money can be withdrawn from *Account No. 1* in dollars or in other currencies. This procedure was also set up in the *Anglo-American Loan Agreement*, since the British *Pound Sterling* was to be freely convertible from 15 July 1947 on. The convertibility of the sterling led to a sterling crisis on 29 August 1947, at which time free convertibility was suspended. The British currency was under pressure since it was unsupported in the economy by an equivalence in production. Thus, access for India was only of a mostly theoretical nature.

The *sterling* began to lose in value. British repayment of debts to the United States and the reconstruction of the economy led to an exploding amount of money. India paid for its imports from the United States on a US-dollar basis in exchange for *Pound Sterling*.

The US-dollar deficit of the Indian government for the second half of 1947 was $60 million. The Indian government's import programme from the United States consisted of mainly food imports, but also other goods worth $100 million. The dollar-crisis in 1947 led to a strict currency control, and the *Pound Sterling* came under pressure because of the outflow of dollars.

7 Indo-British Economic Relations after India's Independence

Great Britain, with the help of the United States, had set up an indirect rule in the sector of financial policy in South Asia for the time after Indian independence. Now attention was directed to the general economic situation in India, foreign trade and Indian trade products.

On 15 August 1947, India received its independence. The *transfer of power* was effectively finished. A constitutional assembly took up its work. A draft of a new constitution was worked out by a committee, and it was hoped that this could be ratified by 1949. Until the final ratification of a new constitution for India, for the developing Indian Union, the quasi-constitution of 1935, the *Government of India Act*, remained in power. The new constitution foresaw a dual division of powers in a federation. A federal government was counterbalanced by the governments of 26 states in the federation. The economic significance of the new constitution could be seen in a number of points:

- Consequences for the financial resources of the federal government and of the states.
- Consequences for economic development and for the federal parliament, the legislative branch, and for the state parliaments.
- The economic consequences of a state of emergency.
- Regulation of trade between the states of the federation.
- Establishment of a unified code of law for all of India.

In Great Britain, the Board of Trade and the *Commonwealth Relations Office* were observing the development of the Indian constitution.

The draft of the new constitution granted the basic rights of equality, religious freedom, cultural freedom, education, property and legal regress in a court system. The government was responsible to

- preserve, protect and promote the well-being of the people
- protect rights to work and education
- set up fair and humane conditions of work.
- guarantee workers a minimum wage and a minimum standard of living
- introduce a unified civil code for India
- guarantee elementary education to all people
- compensate for economic disadvantages among the people
- raise the general standard of living and secure the general supply of food and medical care for the people.

Converting these ideals of the constitution presupposed a strengthening of the economy, which would also be visible in foreign trade relations.

More exact statistical information on India's foreign trade relations should be considered with reservation. Shortages in shipping capacities during the war and the lack of available currency immediately after the war were factors that distorted the picture of India's economic relations.

Total Trading

Exports and imports rose in 1947/48 by 31% compared to 1946/47. The negative balance of trade increased by 36% in 1947/48 compared to 1946/47 owing primarily to increased importing of food. Re-exports sank 15%, whereby governmental purchases alone accounted for Rs. 11 Crores of the Rs. 19 Crores in re-exports.

Exports and Imports of Indian goods in 1947/48

Exports

Exports of Indian goods increased to Rs. 395 Crores in 1947/48 from Rs. 298 Crores in 1946/47. Major export articles were: raw jute, jute thread and jute products, raw cotton, cotton thread and cotton goods, tea, pelts and furs, cooking oil, mineral oil and animal fat, rubber, varnish, resin, seeds and non-metal products.

There was a striking increase in exports of jute thread and jute products, tea, raw cotton, oils and seeds; on the other hand, exports fell for cotton thread, cotton goods, furs and pelts.

Imports

Import volume increased from Rs. 357 Crores in 1946/47 to Rs. 485 Crores in 1947/48. Imports of food rose strongly.

Where did Indian Export Articles Go?

51% of total exports went to *Commonwealth* countries. The volume for 1947/48 was almost identical to that of 1946/47. India's most important trading partners after independence were: Great Britain, the United States, Australia, South Africa and Sri Lanka. These countries imported 77% of India's total exports. In 1948, Australia and Great Britain outstripped the post-war powerhouse United States in trading with India.

Important goods came from the United States, Great Britain, Egypt, Burma, Switzerland, Canada, Kenya, Australia and Italy. These countries accounted for

82% of India's total imports. The United States delivered twice as much wheat to India in 1947/48, compared to 1946/47. The Indian government attempted unsuccessfully to curb imports from the United States as these were causing a shortage of dollars in the *Empire-Dollar-Pool*.

Trade Policies

In his statement on Indian trade policies after independence, the Indian Minister of Trade, together with the *Import Advisory Council*, explained in March 1949 the introduction of import restrictions. The British-Indian government had already introduced import controls once, in 1940, to prevent an unnecessary outflow of dollar reserves and other hard currencies during the war. In 1946 the government liberalised import controls so that consumer goods and investment goods could be imported. The so-called *Open General Licence* system was expanded to include *sterling* imports. The volume of imports reached Rs. 1000 Crores by the end of the fiscal year on 31 March 1947. Imports were decreasing India's currency reserves, especially dollar reserves. This led anew to import controls, this time with the stipulation, that goods could only be imported when counterbalanced by products of equivalent value made in India. In July 1947 the situation got worse. Import controls were linked to currency controls. The negative balance of payments at the end of 1947 forced the government to add further restrictions of imports, especially of those from hard-currency countries. Consumer goods were banned for a period of twelve months. Even raw materials from hard-currency countries were subject to control. Industrial machinery and machine parts were excepted. The trade deficit with hard-currency countries was stopped using these measures. A surplus in the balance of payments with soft-currency countries was used to import important consumer goods. The import controls were loosened in July 1948 and trading continue under normal conditions. In March 1949, in an address to parliament, the Indian Minister of Trade explained that trading policy was oriented over the long run to competition between industrial powers.

More than one simple cause is needed to explain the failure of this policy.

Export Policies of the Indian government

In 1948/49 India was especially dependent on exports to pay for its imports of food. India was also dependent on steel and non-ferrous metals. High levels of both producer goods and consumer goods were still necessary to satisfy demand and to curb the heating up of inflation.

The system of *Export Licences* was changed from time to time, and there were numerous attempts to influence this government procedure. After the partition of British-India, Indian refugees tried to receive a special status. Numerous applicants for an *External Trade Licence* made use of their special status and sold permission to third parties.

Foreign Trade Relations

Trade relations were maintained by India after independence with Western Germany, with Yugoslavia, Pakistan and Japan. In the first half of 1949, India signed new commercial treaties with Italy, France, Belgium, Switzerland, the USSR, Poland, Finland, Austria, Czechoslovakia, Eastern Germany, Hungary, Sweden, Afghanistan, Iran, Iraq, Egypt, Tibet, Thailand, Sri Lanka and Burma.

The commercial treaties signed with these countries were designed to stabilise India's currency and safeguard its programme of economic construction. India was also a part of the international World Trade Organisation network.

India and the World Trade Organisation

India, as creditor of Great Britain, held an important position in this international institution. On 24 March 1948, the member nations of the United Nations' World Trade Conference closed ceremonies with the signing act in Havana. The committee preparing this conference met in London from October to December 1946. The Indian delegation was occupied with items to be settled that concerned participation of the state in the economy and the structure of the ITO executive council. Further items on the agenda were drafts for the signing act which concerned investments in economic development, participation of state in economic development, and discriminating trade restrictions. A number of articles in the signing act affected the economic and trade policies of independent India.
Article 12 – international investments for economic development
Article 13 – government subventions for economic development
Article 18a – discriminatory restrictions of merchant fleets, and on the nature of credit and insurance
Article 75 – structure of the executive commission
Article 94 – general exemptions

India signed the treaty in June 1948 and put the customs regulations into force on 8 July 1948. International trade was hit hard by a recession in the United States. The recession had its effects on both the British and the Indian financial and business markets. The recession caused a drop in British dollar reserves. Reserves fell from £147 million in the first quarter of 1948 to £82 million in the first quarter of 1949, and rose in the third quarter of 1949 to £157 million. Great Britain's gold and dollar reserves, at only £406 million, came to their lowest level on 30 June 1949.

Falls in production were also noted for cotton textiles in India. Overall production in this branch of industry was reduced as production fell from 12 to 15% of its all-time high in July 1948; there was a fall in production of sacking of 25%. However, in other branches things looked better. Outputs of steel, 126,411 tons in March and 117,220 tons in April were above average levels for the decade between 1939 and 1949. The cement and electronics industries were also looking up.

The industrial region of Calcutta in Bengal is worth special attention. Political unrest made economic development more difficult in a region that had to cope with significant structural problems. A lack of investments and low demand produced a recession in this region.

India's balance of trade with Great Britain and with the United States deteriorated. For the period between 1 April 1948 and 31 March 1949, Indian imports worth $600 million were only offset by Indian exports to hard-currency countries worth 390 million. Alone the imports of food and railway locomotives from dollar-block countries came to $180 million.

Indian Balance of Trade and Balance of Payments

In the first half of 1948 the Indian balance of payments was still level, but in each of the third and fourth quarters it deteriorated by Rs. 6 Crores into a minus. From the beginning of 1949, the deficit was enlarged monthly by Rs. 18 Crores. Maritime trade produced a minus of Rs. 95Crores in 1949.

Reasons for the increasing deficit were the premature repeal of the *Open General Licence No. XIV* in May 1948 and the introduction of the *Open General Licence XV*. These worsened the economic framework of things. Import programmes were cut, especially imports from the dollar-block. This affected first of all food imports such as wheat, floor, rice, millet, maize, barley, semolina and spelt. Things had looked different during the war. Agrarian production was at a high during the time between 1942 and 1944/45. This was absolutely necessary for the war effort. Indian industry was activated only at the end of the war in 1944/45; the year 1945/46 registered an extreme index as huge amounts of war material became necessary for the Far Eastern theatre of war.

For the year 1946, the Ministry for Industry and Supplies published only the results of industrial production in British-India outside the later area of Pakistan and outside the principalities in the first census made after the war. The legal basis for this census consisted of the *Industrial statistics act, 1942* and the *"Factories Act, 1934, section 2(j), section 5(l)*. Criteria used were total value of goods produced and cost of goods produced.

In order to finance its foreign trade, India after independence would have to have access to greater currency reserves.

India's Currency Reserves

One source of currency reserves for the Indian government consisted of the British *sterling debts*. The Anglo-American loan agreement specified that a portion of the *Sterling Balances* would have to be released in July 1947 and that debts would have to be paid off starting in 1951. The Indo-British financial agreement of 14 August 1947 postponed payment of Britain's debts to India until 1952. The total amount of British debt was Rs. 1600 Crores, not including the amount that was released in July 1947. The rest of this money was subject to an interest rate of one percent until the year 1951. Subtracted from this money were India's obligations to pay for yearly pensions to British subjects and investment goods in India. It was decided not to let currency reserves grow to more than Rs. 250 Crores.

The amount of currency reserves in India did not make it possible to realise the full extent of India's import programme. Import restrictions and rising demand for consumer goods had to be balanced out.

To put the planning figures of the *Bombay Plan* into effect, Rs. 760 Crores would have been necessary for the first five-year plan. Added together, the economic plans of the Indian central government and the Indian provincial governments came to Rs. 1345 Crores in required funds.

India could not avoid making debts with the International Monetary Fund. Great Britain and the United States were not willing to allow the accumulated wartime debts of the Allies in India to be used as investment money needed to develop the country economically and put economic plans into action. This has been adequately demonstrated.

India's deficit has been estimated at Rs. 88 Crores per year for the period between 1947 and 1952. It was the result of imports of raw materials, investment goods and consumer goods. The annual deficit was reduced by the one percent interest rate on Britain's *sterling debts*, which brought Rs. 15 Crores per year into the treasury. India, however, had to come up with Rs. 25 Crores per year to pay off foreign credits at the International Monetary Fund. The deficit resulted from the amount of *Sterling Balances* that had been released by the Anglo-

American loan agreement, the reserves of 'hard' currency and the quotas on current credit from the International Monetary Fund and other foreign creditors.

From 1948 to 1951, of the amount of *Sterling Balances* agreed to be released, not all of it could not be called into use because of a crisis in the British economy. Under these circumstances, India could only take out Rs. 200 Crores in 1948 from the *Sterling Balances*; it had to borrow Rs. 166 Crores from the International Monetary Fund and use up Rs. 60 Crores of its own currency reserves to finance its ongoing import programme.

In 1947 the deficit amounted to Rs. 440 Crores. In taking foreign loans, India was able to balance out the deficit for the year 1947 using available reserves. Should the reserves not be sufficient, according to the *Eastern Economist*, then imports would also decline. Imports depended on the amount of currency reserves. In the Indo-British financial agreement of 14 August 1947, India waived British repayment of the *sterling debts* at the time of independence and accepted a moratorium. It is quite possible that Great Britain was under pressure from the United States when it worked out the financial agreement with India; Britain probably threatened that the *Sterling Area* would collapse, should the negotiations fail. In fact, this danger did exist. The *Pound Sterling* creditor nations feared for their currency reserves, which they needed to finance the necessary import programmes.

The volume of Indian imports of finished goods depended on a number of factors:

- the unclear political situation in India
- the cost of principle articles of production in India
- the extent of a policy of autarky and its effects on imports of consumer goods
- the application of the invisible balance of payments using repatriation of debts and the intake of interest on British *sterling debts*
- gold and silver reserves.

The volume of Indian imports from Great Britain depended on political resentment against Great Britain, on possible boycotting of British products and furthermore on the competitiveness of British products on the global market. Also decisive were the size of Indian currency reserves, excepting the *Pound Sterling*, and the extent to which British business was determined to invest in India.

The import of capital was imperative. The Indians had hoped for a repayment of the British *sterling debts*. To build up their industry and develop the country after independence they were forced to take out loans from the IMF and the World Bank, after Britain refused to repay its debts. Both institutions were created under pressure from the United States. Sir Stafford Cripps supported the initiatives of the United States to establish the International Monetary Fund and the World Bank.

An excerpt from the **BOARD OF TRADE JOURNAL** on 30 November 1946 reflects the changed nature of Indo-British trade. Comparing British exports in the third and fourth quarters of 1946 to those in the same period of 1938 leads to an interesting observation: British-India took first place in the trade statistics of 1946, whereas in 1938 it had only occupied third place. The position of the United States remained almost the same, in 1938 sixth place and in 1946 it fell to seventh.

British interest in India during the phase of the *transfer of power* was affected by various factors. The Anglo-American financial agreement made Great Britain financially dependent on the United States, the development of Britain's economic potential was restrained; the crisis in the economy after the war and Britain's *sterling debts* in India affected the financial handling of British-Indian trade. In order to lead the British economy out of a depression, the British government would have to look for a settlement in the *Sterling Balances* with India.

7.1. Negotiations over the *Sterling Balances* in 1948

After discussing the negotiations over the *Sterling Balances* before the *transfer of power* in August 1947, this section will discuss the resumption of negotiations in the period after independence.

On 1 December 1947 the Indian Minister of Finance announced that a delegation from the British government would be coming to Delhi to negotiate over the *sterling debts*. He himself proposed extending the existing interim agreement from August of the same year until June 1948, and then settling on a permanent agreement on a ministerial level. The Minister of Finance hoped that Indian members of parliament would participate in the approaching negotiations to give the whole thing a wider basis of legitimisation.

There were two articles of interest here written in British newspapers about the negotiations: *Partition in India* in the 10 December 1947 issue of *The Times*, and *India's Sterling Balances* in the 9 December 1947 issue of *The Financial Times*.

These two articles dealt with the future of the *Sterling Balances*. The Indian Minister of Finance stated his position on the *Sterling Balances* and foreign currency holdings during a parliamentary budget debate on 27 November 1947. *Sterling* holdings had decreased during the previous 18 months by Rs. 1.8 million Crores. The government's standpoint was to use the remaining *Sterling* reserves for buying agrarian and industrial goods for building up the economy. Import restrictions were showing effects in the transfer of capital. From July to November 1947, reserves in London fell by Rs. 210 million. From September 1939 to March 1947, India had paid Rs. 920 million in hard-currency into the *Empire-Dollar-Pool*, the equivalent of $275 million. In 1946/47 India had a deficit of Rs. 220 million in hard-currency, and from April to June 1947 the net deficit increased by another Rs. 150 million. The Indian government's policies for the year 1947 had been aimed to reach an almost balanced position in the balance of payments. Predictions for 1948 were not possible, since the current Indo-British financial agreement ended on 31 December 1947 and further developments were not foreseeable at the time. Taking the dollar crisis into consideration, not only was Great Britain affected, but also other countries that carried on trading on a dollar basis. The Indian Minister of Finance was counting on a quick begin to negotiations with the British over the continuing problem of the *Sterling Balances*.

The new round of negotiations began in December 1947, and the finishing of a new agreement was completed at the beginning of 1948. The 'provisional' agreement of 14 August 1947 ran out on 14 February 1948. For all practical purposes, the August 1947 agreement was prolonged with a few changes until July 1948.

The views of the press were reflected by *The Statist*, a trade and finance journal. Viewed politically, The Statist is closer to the British position than to the Indian. The paper wrote in the 29 November 1947 issue that Indian sterling assets blocked at the *Bank of England* and other banks would not be reduced in order to finance continuing currency transactions. Great Britain was limited its imports of food from the United States to save dollar reserves. The Indian sterling assets lay in the *Bank of England* to cover British debts in the United States. The British Treasury explained that sterling assets of Pakistan and India invested by the Reserve Bank of India came to £1.3 billion on 5 April 1946. By April 1947, they had fallen by £100 million, and in the second quarter of 1947 by another £22 million. India had a deficit with the United States, a slight surplus with Canada and a large trade deficit with Argentina. The Indian import programme was overdrawn, especially the import of consumer goods, which were set by contract. The Indian balance of payments deficit for the second half of 1947 was £48.5 million.

The following facts were the background for the Indian position during negotiations over the British sterling assets:

1. All Indian foreign currency reserves were held in London.
2. During the war, India had made a net gain in dollars; later deficits in buying on the basis of the US dollar. Proving that India had paid more into the *Sterling Area Pool* than it had taken out is difficult.
3. Fears were growing over India's dollar claims for the year 1948. Statistics on India's economy were disconcerting. India was paying six times as much after the war for rice imports from Burma as before the war.
4. Only after 30 September 1948 would it be possible to divide common sterling assets between Pakistan and India.

An obstacle in the negotiations was the amount of*Sterling Balances.*

The negotiations over a possible permanent agreement took place in Delhi in January and February 1948, and in the summer of the same year in London. Negotiations were aimed at balancing out India's US dollar deficit. As in the 1947 negotiations, the British negotiators had arranged to use India's balance of payments as an argument. Also as in 1947, it was successfully linked to the threat of a collapse in the British *Pound Sterling Area Systems.*

Britain's Secret Negotiations with Pakistan and India in the Spring of 1948

A memorandum of the *Overseas Negotiations Committee* maintained that India and Pakistan had received from the *sterling assets* in London £30 million in 1947 as financial funding and £35 million from July to December 1947 as direct repayment. The Indian negotiators wanted to have £15 of this in US dollars to pay for imports from the United States. At the *Sterling Area* conference in October 1947, the Indian and Pakistani delegations were not authorised to negotiate over the dollar saving measures of their countries. The governor of the Reserve Bank of India, Deshmukh, pointed out to the delegations that no access to the pool would be possible in the first half of 1948, and referred to the International Monetary Fund as financial source for the industrial policies of both governments. Both the Indian and the Pakistani governments refused to take on loans from the IMF until the question of financing Australian wheat deliveries and other goods from the *Sterling Area* had been clarified.

In 1947, because of India's chronicle deficit in US dollar reserves, the Indian government tried to withdraw £35 million from the *sterling pool*. The Indian government did not accept the British condition that they take on a loan from the IMF to make up for the difference to the £15 million actually paid out. The negotiations between Great Britain and India clarified the dispute over the British *sterling debts* and the Indian US dollar deficit. The solution was seen in prolonging a modification of the 14 August 1947 agreement until 14 August 1948. It was to be automatically prolonged every six months by another six months unless one of the parties to the agreement gave notice.

In the spring of 1948, Great Britain was not yet ready for long-term permanent agreements with India and the other creditor nations. What did Britain's willingness to pay off its *sterling debts* depend on? At the end of the war, Great Britain was caught up in a crisis of the economy and its currency.

7.2. British Economic and Currency Crisis

Situation in India

In the course of the Second World War, India gained dollar reserves; these were given over to the British currency control office. These were then available to all members of the entire *sterling block*. India received *Pound Sterling* as counter to this.

At the end of 1943, the British and Indian governments agreed that India would receive for its exports to the United States a yearly $20 million balancing of transfer payments to the *Sterling Area*. Both sides considered this agreement as compensation for India's part in extending *Reciprocal Aid*; the later was a means of supplying the United States during the war with raw materials and food for combat units. Two sums of $20 million for the years 1944 and 1945 were viewed by both parties to the agreement as a basis for building Indian industry after the war. The Indian government did not consider these amounts as enough for payments transferred to the *Empire-Dollar-Pool* . But the British government refused to consider further concessions. The other Empire countries only had access to the *dollar pool* after the end of hostilities with Japan. Obligatory payments to the United States from the common *Empire-Dollar-Pool* preceded access to the British dollar reserves.

A report by the British Treasury on the negotiations between Great Britain and the Indian government indicated that the Pakistani and Indian common currency fund would not be split before 30 September 1948. The reason for this was the weak position of the *Pound Sterling* and the poor economic situation of Great Britain.

Great Britain's economy was ruined at the end of World War Two. Here are a few facts and figures as proof.

It was only in 1950 that Great Britain regained its pre-war level of economic productivity. To continue the war effort, the British economy had been dependent on foreign credit and supplies of aid from 1942 on. The resulting debts were to be repaid at the end of the war, which, as it finally came in the summer of 1945, caused severe economic problems for Great Britain. The figures for Britain's trade deficit were catastrophic. The huge mountain of imports worth $1540 billion were hardly counterbalanced by a miserable heap of British exports worth $340 million. The situation was made worse by the decrease in dollar reserves in the *Sterling Area*. The energy crisis of 1947 and the economic crisis of the *Pound Sterling* weakened the structural framework of the British economy. The *Pound Sterling* was devaluated in September 1949 in comparison to the dollar by more than a fourth, from $4.03 to $2.80.

As early as June 1945, before the end of the war in the Pacific, there were signs that the *Pound Sterling* would be devaluated against the dollar. R.W.B. Clarke wrote in a memorandum about the crushing burden on Britain and the effects on consolidating the budget and British foreign trade. The *Pound* was at a disadvantage in trade with other hard-currency countries. Leading economists in the United States pressed for a devaluation of the British *Pound*. British dollar reserves fell rapidly after the war. The British Treasurer Sir Stafford Cripps warned that it would be necessary to correct trade or currency policies.

At the *Commonwealth Conference* in July 1949, a cut of 25% in the dollar import programme were decided on for one year, until July 1950. The decision was kept to. However, the United States pressed Great Britain to reduce the government quota and to stop the nationalisation of important primary energy sectors such as mining, electricity and water. The deficits in the balance of payments increased to over £240 million yearly by 1949.

What effects did Great Britain's economic decline have on Indo-British economic relations? The part of the *Sterling Balances* has been adequately discussed.

7.3. Imports and Exports: Great Britain and the *Dominion of India*

The import and export policies of Great Britain and the Dominion of India were determined by various factors. Factors for India's economic forecast for 1947 to 1952 are listed below, with favourable and unfavourable factors contrasted.

Unfavourable factors for continuing with India's economic development were the absence of the *Sterling Balances* for a boost in financing the economy and for industrial development. After the war, India was hit by a severe recession. The reduction of secret currency reserves for urgently needed imports worsened the balance of trade and turned it into negative figures. Another difficulty was foreign financing of economically important industrial projects.

Other factors were the currency controls of the Indian government and the poor condition of gold and precious metal reserves. The prospects were not optimistic for industrial development.

Favourable factors for India's import and export policies were the elimination of the danger of war in India and the prospect of international industrial development aid in Asia. Economically viewed, India had overcame the recession in industrial production. A three-year plan to secure provisions for the Indian population made an expansion of the agrarian economy inevitable. The expansion in the railway network and thus in the Indian infrastructure was good for economic development. State intervention in the economy was justified at first, but mismanagement and corruption negated what had been a good start. The Indian government was faced with political opposition in its own country. In addition, the government had an aversion to private business.

The analysis led to the conclusion that for the economic development of India in the period from 1947 to 1952, unfavourable factors outweighed favourable ones. The significance of the unfavourable factors would grow in importance over the long run. What, however, was the prediction for concrete sectors? A study by the India Office was useful for both optimistic and pessimistic assessments of Indian imports over the same period of time. The study's statistics were used by the Indians for determining imports and calculating the country's currency reserves; the same statistics were used by the British for calculations and tactics at the negotiations over the *Sterling Balances*.

Gandhi's idea of a self-sufficient economy did not have much influence on the Indian government's development of economic plans. The government was far more interested in getting certain projects started and commissioning the necessary foreign companies to do so. The government was deciding which of these capital-intensive industrial branches should be promoted. The Indian cotton textile industry was one of those that came into consideration. An increase of 50% in this sector was envisioned. The government's programme consisted of transferring capital and providing the Indian textile industry with orders for the decade up to 1957.

The Indian government planned to continue the development of primary energy supplies. Technological construction and training of technical operators was to take place during the time up until 1950. Another ambitious governmental project was to increase production of sugar by 15%. Licensing the urgently needed technology went on until 1950, and construction of factories until 1952.

The Indian government's import programme was quite comprehensive and designed to extend existing branches of industry such as jute products, paper, steel, glass, machinery, consumer goods machinery, construction materials and road construction machinery.

The government's plans included a number of wishes for new branches of industry, including automobile production, as foreseen by the *Nuffield-Birla Agreement*, rayon production, irrigation systems and artificial fertiliser plants. To fight the food shortage problem and reduce the importing of food from foreign countries, the Indian government wanted to promote the agriculture business, improve irrigation systems and fight against crop failures.

At the same time, the India Office was making a pessimistic assessment of India's import policy.

The India Office made the following assumptions in working out their assessment: Political conflicts within India could have a negative effect on trade and on industry and foreign trading partners would lose faith in dealing with India.

This assessment was based on various sources of information on trade with India, information that served the industrial build-up of the country, for example guidelines to the so-called *Bombay Plan*. Thus, for the cotton textile industry and for the chemical industry, the following factors were important:

A drop in prices for Indian raw materials and a permanent avoidance of British imports for certain branches of industry that were extended or newly set up during the war, these were two such factors. A third factor was the failure of the Indian government's programmes for solving the food, work and health problems of the Indian population. An increase in nepotism was endangering the fundamentals of trade.

Nationalising British businesses in India would have severe effects on import policies. Among those affected would be British exports to India that depended on the political views of the Indian government and on those of British industry. The India Office went on to ask whether British industry was competitive enough for the purpose of trading with India, and to ask to what bearing the amount of India's hard-currency reserves had on the balance of payments; these were further factors that led the India Office to a pessimistic assessment of Indian imports.

This assessment shows, of course, the British point of view. A comparable study showing the Indian point of view was not available.

What was the situation for British trading with India at the time? *The Financial Times* printed an article on this subject on 4 June 1947, 'Britain's Trade in and with India'. The point of time this article appeared was interesting, as the Indian government published its so-called *3 June Plan* on the same day. This plan shortened the process of the *transfer of power* and set the date for independence at 15 August 1947.

The article in the *Financial Times* found a connection between Indo-British trade and the British *Sterling Balances* problem. Many articles appeared on the subject of the *Sterling Balances* at the time, giving an idea of the size of the problem, and, above all, its extent. Not only were India and Great Britain affected, but also the United States and other nations of the *Commonwealth*. Negotiations on this matter were to have effects on the entire *Sterling Area System*.

What were economic relations like between the principalities and Great Britain after British-India's independence?

Exports from the Indian Principalities to Great Britain after India's Independence

A problem for many of the Indian principalities was their geographical location. 'Isolated' geographically, they were forced to transport their export goods across the territory of the newly-created Dominion of India.

Among the principalities, the most important trading partner internationally was Hyderabad. It traded in peanuts, linseed, sesame and cotton. Mysore, another Indian principality, exported wood and coffee. Travancore exported coffee etc. In addition to Great Britain, important trading partners for the principalities were Egypt, the United States, Iran and Iraq.

At the India Office, Thomson doubted that any one of the Indian principalities could become detrimental to the *standstill agreement* between Great Britain and principalities. Viceroy Mountbatten sent a telegram to the Secretary of State for India explaining the situation shortly before independence:

"Commonwealth or international implementation on administrative arrangements made jointly by India and the states. These arrangements are covered by schedule to draft standstill Agreement which includes customs and import and export control. It does not seem possible to go beyond this until

constitutions of the dominions are framed providing for control by federal centre of external relations of all units including the states."

The British Board of Trade also commented on this problem mentioned by the Secretary of State for India. In a memorandum, the Board of Trade attempted to clarify the question of how to handle British imports from the Indian principalities after 15 August 1947.

The following considerations were made to the problem: Could Great Britain grant most-favoured status to the principalities, which, after 15 August 1947, were not allied with either India or Pakistan economically and politically? Could trading be carried on using the present *imperial preferences* as a legal basis, despite the status of the Indian principalities under international law?

To avoid uncertainties, the British Board of Trade issued the following guidelines:

1. How would British policy be shaped for those principalities which had not committed themselves to one of the two dominions by 15 August 1947? According to the guidelines, in the transitional period until final commitment, goods from such Indian principalities were to be treated the same as those subject to British *imperial preferences*. These principalities were to enjoy diplomatic and commercial advantages over third states.
2. How would British policy be shaped for such principalities that should declare themselves sovereign and independent after 15 August 1947? This was already the case with the two principalities Hyderabad and Tranvancore.
3. When should the British government recognise these principalities as sovereign states?
4. When would the new Indian government under Nehru set its annexation policy into practice? The Board of Trade was of the opinion that principalities seeking independence after 15 August 1947 should be recognised under international law.

These questions were to be understood in connection with negotiations of the World Trade Organisation taking place in Geneva. Articles of the WTO *charta* affecting British interests were amended so that Great Britain could maintain its bilateral *preferences* within the Empire, even if India or Burma, despite negotiations over multilateral trade relations, should leave the *Commonwealth*. In a appendix to the *charta*, the various territories of the British Empire were listed, including India and Burma. As Burma and India had reserved the right to leave the *Commonwealth* and thus to exit from the system of British *preferences*, in this way the Indian principalities could choose to leave the *Commonwealth* as sovereign states after 15 August 1947 and nonetheless remain voting members of the World Trade Organisation.

Despite independence from Great Britain under international law, these states were further economically and commercially connected to the system of British *preferences*, even if they should depart the *Commonwealth*, and they would continue to enjoy the advantages of their previous participation in the British Empire.

The India Office worked carefully together with the British Board of Trade, and proceeded in a highly tactical and diplomatic manner with the principalities seeking independence under international law. They almost succeeded in creating for Great Britain an additional commercial option for transacting trade with countries in South Asia and Southeast Asia that would have improved its status as competitor to the United States, and this, although contrary to treaty agreements with the United States – the Anglo-American loan agreement of December 1945, the *Lend-Lease Act* of 1942, and *article seven* of the *Mutual Aid Agreement* of February 1942.

In spite of debt and a weak economy after the Second World War, Great Britain, with the help of the Indo-British *Financial Agreement* of 14 August 1947, was able to reach a position of financial and economic supremacy and thus influence and even dictate the nature of Indo-British economic relations after 1947.

8 Synthesis of Political and Economic Factors in Indo-British Economic Relations from 1939 to 1950

Entanglement of politics and economy

Forming a synthesis between the political and economical factors in the tangle of Indo-British relations is not an easy task. The political, social, economic and legal conditions of the two countries are far too different. Yet in order to achieve a credible synthesis, an attempt will be made using the facts available to form a picture which can serve as an explanatory model.

Facts, problems and solutions

The 1930s were marked by severe economic crises and their repercussions. The world-wide depression starting in 1929 should be taken into consideration here. In 1931, the gold parity of the *Pound sterling* was abandoned. A series of protectionist measures undertaken by the British government as emergency brake were supposed to counter-balance the deteriorating commercial figures resulting from the *laissez-faire* policy and the free trade doctrine. In 1932, the Conference of Ottawa revealed the impracticability of neomercantilism. It became necessary to introduce a protective customs and tariffs system, the *Imperial Tariffs and Preferences*. The resolutions made at the Ottawa Conference changed Indo-British commercial relations at the expense of India. The Imperial Preferences assured Great Britain a sales market for its trade products in economically difficult times at conditions favourable for Britain. A detailed list of goods with a mutual preference guarantee was agreed upon at the Ottawa Conference. At the same time, the currency was depreciated in order to increase the export figures outside the Empire. The bilateral commercial relations between Great Britain and its contracting parties as well as the discriminating preferences practice did not, however, bring about any long-term improvement in the *Empire* economic system, nor in Great Britain's trade balance deficit. Both Great Britain's borrowing policy and indebtedness during the Second World War and the post-war era led equally to destabilisation.

Here politics intervened in economic processes. That is, a policy of regulation was pursued to protect the home market, the export economy and national currency stability. The British cotton textile production in Lancashire, for example, was protected by the *Lees-Mody Pact* of October 1933. Further protective measures included the *Indian Tariff (Textiles Protection) Amendment Act of 1934*, the *Indian Tariff Second Amendment Act of 1939*, and *the Indian Tariff Third Amendment Act of 1939*. The cotton question was ignored during the Ottawa Conference negotiations. The British government was rightly afraid of political demands by the Indian liberation movement and thus aimed to reach an agreement that satisfied all parties involved. The agreement reached, the *Ottawa Trade Agreement*, as well as other bilateral trade agreements that Great Britain settled with *Empire* counties and other contracting nations, saved the British economy from ruin and the British state from insolvency. These agreements led to political disputes in the signatory countries. Within Indian industrial circles there was an uproar over the conference results and the conditions under which economic politics were imposed. The criticism was directed against the plan laid down in these agreements proposing to turn the Empire into a single economic zone with dependent areas of lesser rights, against economic and political protectionism, and against Great Britain's dictatorship as colonial power in the trade agreements. The question of how to legally safeguard trade with third states led to controversial debates and resolutions in the Indian Parliament. A new Indo-British trade agreement became necessary, not least due to the political protests. The Lancashire cotton lobby urged that an agreement be reached quickly. A speedy conclusion of such an agreement failed, however, due to the unyielding standpoints of the various interest groups - the Moslem League, the National Congress and the European Group.

The beginning of the Second World War and the conversion to a war economy represented a turning point in Indo-British commercial relations. The **Economic Resources Board** was set up as a political instrument to implement and promote control measures imposed by the wartime economy. Its responsibilities included working out import licences and the **Open General Licences**.

When the Indian National Congress refused to co-operate economically, the Indian Minister Amery reacted by refusing to continue with the question of a constitution for India. Economic demands were bound directly together with political and constitutional concessions. Yet these concessions were not enough to alter the precarious situation. Irreversible government intervention in the course of the economy was called for. This intervention was supposed to stimulate the British export economy and largely leave exchange reserves untouched. Neither of these actually happened.

The representatives of the Indian government and the representatives of the Indian industry negotiated on their trade interests, including, among other things, the costs of production goods in the wartime economy. Great Britain tried to gain influence on pricing by way of the government in Delhi and recommended price control measures in order to keep British *sterling* debts down for the Indians. Despite being bound by directives, the government of India complained about the import control regulations laid down by the British government and called these political protectionism in the economic sector. The same applied to financial and monetary controls. Here Britain intervened in India in the person of the British representative, the viceroy, who referred to the emergency article of the *Government of India Act, 1935*. In 1941, the United States and Great Britain signed a lend-lease agreement to assure wartime production. The lend-lease goods negotiated in this agreement were put under the control of agencies and institutions loyal to the government. Matters of wartime economy were decided by politics. In this way, customs and the amount levied by customs tariffs had the selective effect of regulative measures on import and export trading activities. Indian critics saw India as the "victim of the British economic imperialism". The financing of trade between India and third counties was controlled by the British government through the newly founded ***United Kingdom Commercial Corporation***. This control contradicted Britain's demand on Indian industry to share more of the wartime expenses. The Indian economy 'revolted'. But it had to give in to British dictates.

The extremes of Indian export policy and of the wartime industry during the Second World War had disastrous consequences on domestic affairs in India. Political riots and supply bottlenecks resulted from the wartime economy. In order to bind India nevertheless to Britain as a source of foreign currency and as producers of war goods, economic plans were drawn up at the end of the war to develop Indian industry in the post-war era. On the Indian side was the *Bombay Plan* of leading Indian industrialists and the *Roy Plan*. Facing these on the British side were the *Cripps-Bevin Plan* and the official plan of the Indian government. Indo-British commercial and trade relations were severely strained by Great Britain's financial burden in the form of the *sterling balances*.

As to why the British creditor states, including India, agreed to the *sterling* moratorium – for it was nothing more than that – in 1947 and in the years following, this can only be explained by the common interest that these states had in the economic stability of Great Britain. They did not want to decrease the value of British sterling debts, as this money, after all, belonged to the creditors.

Is it conceivable that Dr. Gregory, the British economic adviser in India, co-operated with the Indian liberation movement in the post-war era? Such an assumption could be supported by the common interest of both the British and the

Indian side in a united, independent Indian nation. The common interest was based on the good Indo-British trade and economic relations. These were important to Nehru for the time after India's independence. Nehru demanded not only the political unity of India, but also that it be a unified economic area, as only economic unity can pave the way for a strong political unity. Since Nehru and the British viceroy Lord Mountbatten co-operated well enough politically, the conclusion is justified that they also co-operated relatively well in questions of trade and economy. It must also not be forgotten that the British were competitors to the Americans in South Asia.

India's independence was linked to the *sterling* debts of the British and the credit policy pursued by the United States. The US exerted direct and indirect influence on Indo-British negotiations over the *sterling balances*. In the Anglo-American financial agreement of December 1945, as far back as the Anglo-American trade agreement of 1938 as well as in the Anglo-American *Lend-Lease Agreement* of 1941, the US required Great Britain to play an active part in the haggling over a reduction of Britain's debt to its creditors. India not only was a victim of British economic imperialism, but also of the financial entanglements between Great Britain and America. In the reorganisation of world economy and world trade after the Second World War, the United States placed the accents, not least as counterpoint to the emerging economic block under Soviet-Russian domination and to the beginning phase of the Cold War. The International Monetary Fund (I.M.F.) and the Bank for Reconstruction and Development (IBRD) were established as a result of the Bretton Woods Conference. The new institutions remained within the hegemonic interests of the United States.

Along with the economic co-operation between British and Indian leaders of industry, there was also political agreement on constitutional questions. Nevertheless, a number of British investors were frightened off by political events in India. Gandhi sharply criticised Indian economic co-operation with the British. Yet, in spite of his disapproval, economic co-operation worked quite well, as the Birla-Nuffield agreement shows. During the Second World War, in the economic sector of aviation, Tata Ltd. and the India Office had already co-operated politically and commercially.

Although the United States and Great Britain co-operated as allies during the war, they competed for trade positions on the Indian sub-continent in the post-war era. The influence of the United States was evident in the course of the negotiations for the Anglo-American bond agreements and quite obvious during the related Indo-British negotiations for a *financial settlement* in the spring of

1947. Indo-British economic and financial relations were victimised by the maelstrom of post-war Anglo-American economic and financial relations.

The British Treasury wanted to prevent this during the war. A plan was worked out to promote exports to India in order to reduce the accumulation of debt. These British repayment plans were thwarted by US trade interests in India. Politics and economic matters were mixed into the constitutional issue in India and into the so-called 'Transfer of Power'.

After the *Labour Party's* take-over of power, the British expected a solution to structural problems of the economy, and Indians a solution to India's constitutional question. A solution to the Indian constitutional question was reached by way of a compromise in the question of British debt. The British dismissed India into its political independence. In return, they expected of India a willingness to compromise and make concessions in the negotiations of the *sterling balances*.

Is the moratorium of the *sterling balances* conceivable as the political catalyst? In concrete terms: Is the *Financial Agreement* of 14 August 1947 conceivable as the 'price' for the *India Independence Act, 1947* of 15 August 1947?

In the spring of 1947, the British export industry tried to exert an increasing influence on the negotiations for the *transfer of power*. To secure its commercial interests in India, the British business community wanted to establish economic relations to India without prior agreement as to the political framework. This was a departure from the negotiating position adopted at the Ottawa Conference in 1932. This position presupposed a judicial framework as binding basis of legitimacy for economic relations: "*Industrialisation on stable political foundation*", as a representative of the Indian economic delegation stated in London on 20 June 1945.

The reaction in Great Britain was very different. The British Treasury prohibited the Indian government in Delhi during the post-war era from spending dollars on important imports from the United States and other states in the *dollar area*. British politicians could rely on Indian loyalty by putting on the thumb screws. British industry insisted that the British government conclude a new trade agreement before finishing negotiations for India's political independence. The British government warned against such steps, as no agreement in terms of the *sterling* debts could be expected before India was granted independence. Insistence on constitutional 'safeguards' made the transfer of power to the Indians all the more difficult. This wrangling over the *Safeguarding Sections* of the *Government of India Act, 1935, Art. 111-121* marked the atmosphere prevailing in the India Office and in the British government in the early spring of 1947. The pressure group of British industry, the *Joint Committee on India*, fiercely defended British economic interests in India and insisted on retaining the *safeguards*. They enabled British entrepreneurs in India to establish subsidiaries with the designation 'India Limited'. These were then favoured by customs and could compete with native Indian establishments on equal terms. Behind the wall of preferential customs set up as an instrument of economic recovery by the Ottawa Conference and accepted by the nations participating, the signatory nations assumed undisturbed indigenous industrial development. Using their status, the newly established British companies were able to bypass the protective preferential customs and drove out Indian competitors.

In the phase of transferring power, conflicts arose between the British lobby in India and the political representatives of Indian industry in the negotiations committee *transfer of power*. The Indian minister Dalal, who had been appointed by the British Viceroy and commissioned with the planning and development of the Indian economy in the post-war era, resigned when he realised that he was not able to find a conciliatory compromise between British persistency and the strict refusal of the Indian party to accept the *safeguards*. He was being put under pressure to prevail by the Indian nationalists. They now formed the majority in the Indian Central Parliament after the British had agreed to holding elections in the Indian province parliaments in November 1946, and they would have regarded Dalal's giving in as a betrayal of the *Indian Question* and the independence movement. The inflexible attitude of both sides led to Dalal's resignation. It was not only the *safeguards*, but also the accumulated *sterling balances* which placed a heavy burden on Indian-British commercial relations in the post-war era. How was a solution to the problems ahead to be reached?

The British were keenly interested in trade and exchange with India in the post-war era. On the other side, Indian industrials were just as interested in a productive co-operation with the British, despite political differences. At first, at the end of the war, a delegation of Indian industrials came to Great Britain and the United States in order to negotiate about projects in the form of joint ventures. As *sterling* creditors, the Indians were able to offer cash for Western industrial products. However, the Indian side could not dispose freely of their sterling assets, as they had presumed in their plans for financing Indian industrial development. The entanglement of financial dependency on American credit and the repayment of this credit was a heavy burden for Great Britain. British export opportunities had decreased rapidly in the post-war era. The British economy was devastated. The British people demanded consumer goods after six years of deprivation. The Marshall Plan set up by the United States and the UNRRA aid made it possible for Britain to transform its war-oriented economy to one for producing civilian goods. These goods were designated both for domestic consumption and for export, the latter necessary to procure urgently needed foreign currency. Great Britain sat on a fence. On the one hand, India insisted on the repayment of their sterling deposits in London. By refusing to pay off these debts, Great Britain was able to obstruct the development of Indian industry and thus hinder a future competitor in Asia. On the other hand, the US insisted on the repayment of its credit. Not enough that Great Britain was now debtor both to the United States and to India, it was also being forced out of its entrenched role as a world-wide economic power by the United States. The newly-established institutions which determined the new international economic order, the IMF (International Monetary Fund) and the World Bank, reflected the ideas of the United States and were set up ignoring suggestions made by the British. Regionally, the US was trying to replace Great Britain as the supreme economic power in Southern Asia. This started back in the 1930s with political contact to the Indian national movement and continued diplomatically with the demand in the Atlantic Charter that Great Britain retreat from India. As India's 'natural' ally in its struggle for national independence and Great Britain's economic competitor, the United States was able to promote its own economic interests by espousing 'freedom' and 'right of self-determination' for all peoples. In this respect, Indo-American joint ventures were paving the way. Confronted with the political, economic, financial and monetary superiority of the United States, Great Britain had to pass while the post-war order was being formed, and gave in to the American demand that debts be paid off. Since India wanted to obtain independence and was not economically so strong as the US, since it had only accumulated a sterling fortune during the war not to be underestimated, did not play any role in the world of politics, and during the Second World War had been merely a procurer of foreign currencies and producer of war materials; the chances of its pressuring the British into repaying debts was marginally slim. In addition to this, whether independent or ruled by Great Britain, India needed the sterling fortune it was hoarding. Great Britain might refuse to pay off its debts, arguing a possible collapse of the sterling block, resulting bankruptcy of the British state, and the subsequent and inevitable voiding of Indian demands. There was nothing India could counter these arguments with, and thus it had to accept the moratorium set up by Great Britain.

This situation forced the Indian to take out external loans at the World Bank and the International Monetary Fund. Unfortunately, the prestige projects which the Indian government and Indian industrials planned required India to take up excessive external loans.

The settlement of the sterling debts and the conclusion of the *financial agreements* was achieved using the Egyptian treaty draft as model.

The second problem was more difficult to solve. The constitutional guaranties for British economic interests in India stood in the way of dynamic economic development in India. Thanks to the announcement of the 'Plan of June the 3rd', British exporters faced increasing time pressure to assert their rights as guaranteed in the new constitution.

Time was not on the side of British economic interests in India. In 1942 the British Treasury had warned of excessive sterling expenditures. The ensuing burden of debt would weaken Great Britain's competitive chances in the post-war era.

The British historian Tomlinson attempts to reconstruct the *sterling balances* negotiations between the British and the Indians. However, he fails to connect British dependence on the United States with these sterling negotiations and thus neglects the resulting economic and financial triangle.
The prolongation of British sterling debts must be seen in this context. The British monetary and economic crises of 1947 and 1949 further compounded matters. The British reaction followed time-honoured procedure – restriction of imports and exports and strict monetary policy. In the first phase of India's independence, the British exerted their influence on the Reserve Bank of India. Governor Deshmukh fulfilled double duties for both India and Pakistan until 30 September 1948. He was a loyal champion of British interests overseeing the division of total sterling debts and credits into shares for Pakistan and India.

As a result of these negotiations, it seems that politics and fiscal policy increasingly favoured Great Britain and the West and disfavoured India and thus, Asia.

Parallel to negotiations over the *transfer of power*, as announced by Attlee on 20 February 1947, British and Indian delegations negotiated Indian sterling balances in British hands, as mentioned above. When the prime minister announced British retreat from India, he did not mention British economic interests in India, nor the Indo-British trade agreement, nor the *safeguards* for British business in India. Industrial development in India after the war was not to be encumbered by the *safeguards*. In the spring of 1947, the British business lobby for Indo-British trade felt cheated by the Labour government. Without an

Indo-British trade agreement and without a settlement of the Indian sterling balances, the basis for British business in India was in danger. The Indian side categorically refused to negotiate over a prolongation of the *safeguards*. In the new contract, the *Indian (Independence) Act, 1947*, no preferential position for the British in India was included. During the *transfer of power* negotiations, the British government and the British delegation resisted all pressuring on the part of the 'Indian lobby' – British business interests – to integrate protectionist measures into the constitution. Simultaneously to these two negotiations, the situation was fortified by the effects of the Anglo-American Financial Agreement of December 1945.

The interdependence of Indian independence and the Anglo-American Financial Agreement plus the negotiations over the *sterling balances* is quite obvious. Evidence of this is the American demand that British foreign debts be lowered, and that Britain agree to make concessions in questions of imperial preferential duties and comply with American requests for a liberalisation of world trade.

The facts concerning Indo-British economic relations in the period of 1939 to 1950 lead to the following model of an economic and financial triangle:

The United States is allied with Great Britain by way of trade and credit agreements. This closer link during the Second World War was inevitable, not so intended in its consequences by Prime Minister Churchill, but bound nonetheless so to develop.

Great Britain is bound to the United States by a trade agreement of 1938 and by the war alliance during the Second World War. The British are linked to India by a trade agreement, by political prerogatives and resulting financial dictates in the form of sterling accumulation.

And finally, India is tied to both the United States by trade and credit agreements and 'voluntary' raw material supplies and to Great Britain by British political prerogatives and British trade dominance, and, not in the least, by the unsolved issue of the sterling settlement.

The result of this 'triangle relationship' can be summarised as follows: The unstoppable rise of the United States to world power led to the dependency of Great Britain, which was suffering from the consequences of two world wars. India, having emerged from the war as creditor, could only make limited use of its advantage for the following reasons: Great Britain was forced to impose a moratorium on India because of its dependency on the United States; India was then forced to incur debts with the World Bank and the International Monetary Fund, institutions sustained by the United States.

9 Conclusion

A word at the end of the discussion.

The subtitle of the present work is *British Withdrawal from Asia – Asians Ahead after the First Round?* The question mark here is a deliberate reference to the coming century. The twenty-first century, the Asian century? The next few year will show whether the predictions for growth in the region of Asia will become reality or not, with consequences for Europe, the former colonial power Great Britain and the other Western industrial nations. A continuation of the circuit discussed above might be seen in the return of Crown Colony Hong Kong, fifty years after the British withdrew for financial and economic reasons from South Asia. Hong Kong was returned under pressure from the People's Republic of China, and not just because the 99-year lease ran out. Similar to events 50 years ago, with the *transition period* and the negotiations over the *transfer of power*, Great Britain has secured by treaty a further 50 years of economic privileges in this 'Special Economic Zone' of the People's Republic. There can be no realistic comparison to the *financial settlement* of 1947, however, because Hong Kong has always been a part of China. With Hong Kong, an occupied territory has been returned to a Chinese Republic already in existence.

An Indian nation was first created in 1947. The comparison here involves different political problems and different constitutional questions. British Governor Patton, who remained in office until 1 July 1997, allowed Hong Kong Chinese to participate in the *Executive Council* and in the administration; this was quite like the Indianisation practised by Linlithgow and Wavell during World War Two. Similar to British-India, Hong Kong plays a highly significant economic role, especially in the Far East. As one of the largest Asian financial centres after Tokyo, Hong Kong has been a financial and economic bridgehead for London up to now. Great Britain gave in to the political pressure of the Chinese, as was to be expected. With India in 1947, things were different. The British government did not give in to the political pressure of masses of Indians, nor to the ethnic-religious fighting between Moslems and Hindus. This could have been settled with mutual tolerance and with less religious fanaticism, which would have allowed one unified nation on the Indian subcontinent to confront the supremacy of Western economic interests in South Asia. On the contrary, economy weakness and financial indebtedness were the primary reasons that forced Great Britain in the period between 1918 and 1947 to give up its colony and withdraw from South Asia – as indicated here by the subtitle as working hypothesis from the start.

The present work has attempted to verify this hypothesis – *withdrawal from Asia with retention of Western financial and economic supremacy* – in a number of steps and from a number of aspects. This was done by a three-fold approach to the core of the matter. In the chronological unfolding of events concerning Indo-British economic relations in the period from 1918 to the early 1950s, a historical framework was developed.

The second methodical step lay in presenting Indo-British economic relations from the perspectives of Great Britain as colonial power, the British colonial government in India, British business interests and the colony of India, the latter with its own economic interests and political national movement.

Last but not least, the attempt was made to embed this discussion in a global economic context, the result of the reforms made on global economic trade relations after the war; and to embed it in the global financial dependencies of both parties, India and Britain, after the war.

This results presented here are therefore to be understood as one part of the mosaic of global economic and financial networks; these networks did not first appear per computer and Internet at the end of the century, but made themselves felt back in 1929 with the start of the Great Depression and continued to do so during the period of World War Two, as attentive analysts all over the world are certain to have noticed. Especially this long war, at first an intermezzo in the process of globalisation, became a catalyst for the development of a new world order, a world order that has remained to the present day and that will unfold fully in the following century.

Are the Asians ahead after all?

10 Bibliography

-Adarkar, B.P.: The Indian Fiscal Policy. Allahabad 1941.
-Addison, Paul: Churchill on the Home Front, 1900-1955. London 1992.
-Agarwala, A.N.: Position and Prospects of India's foreign trade. Allahabad 1947.
-Agarwala, P.N.: The history of Indian business. A complete account of trade exchanges from 3000 BC to the present day. New Delhi 1985.
-Ahmad, Z.A.: Some economic and financial aspects of British rule in India. Allahabad 1937.
-All-India Commerce Conference (1947) Lucknow, India's leading commercial problems. Allahabad 1948.
-Ambirajan, S.: Classical political economy and british policy in India. Cambridge 1978.
-Anjaria, J.J.: Price control in India, with special reference to food supply, by J.J. Anjaria, D.T. Lakdawala, D.R. Samant. o.O. 1946.
-Anstey, V.P.: The economic development of India. London 1952 (Vierte Auflage).
-Aster, Sidney: Anthony Eden. British Prime Ministers. London 1976.
-Bachmann, Hans: Die Konvention von Bretton Woods. IWF und Internationale Bank für Wiederaufbau. St. Gallen 1945.
-Banerjea, P.: An introduction to the study of Indian economics. Calcutta 1951.
-Banerjea, P.N.: A study of Indian economics. London 1940 (Fünfte erweiterte Auflage).
-Banerji, Arun Kumar: India's Balance of Payments. Estimates of Current and Capital Accounts from 1921-22 to 1938-39. London 1963.
-Bechtoldt, Heinrich: Indien oder China. Die Alternative in Asien. München 1964.
-Benham, F.: Great Britain under Protection. New York 1941.
-Bhagvati, J./ Desai, P.: Planning for Industrialisation. London 1970.
-Bhagvati, J./ Srinivasan, T.N.: Foreign Trade Regimes and Economic Development in India. New York 1979.
-Bhatt, V.V.: Aspects of economic change and policy in India, 1800-1960. Bombay 1967.
-Bhide, Anant Sadashiv: From quit India to split India. Poona 1945.
-Blondel, Jean: Demokratie in England. Wähler, Parteien, Politiker. Frankfurt am Main 1964.

-Bondurant, Joan V.: Conquest of Violence. The Gandhian Philosophy of Conflict. Princeton 1958.
-Boyle, Andrew: Norman Montagu. London 1967.
-Brecher, Michael: Nehru. A Political Biography. Oxford 1959.
-Bridge, Carl: Holding India to the Empire: The British Conservative Party and the 1935 Constitution. London 1986.
-Brown, Judith M.: Modern India. The Origins of an Asian Democracy. Oxford 1985.
-Cairncross, Alec/ Eichengreen, Barry: Sterling in Decline. The Devaluations of 1931, 1949 and 1967. Oxford 1983.
-Chakravarty, Suhash: The RAJ Syndrome. A Study in Imperial Perceptions. New Delhi 1989.
-Chatterjee, Partha: Nationalist thought and the colonial world: a derivate discourse? New Delhi 1986.
-Chatterji, Basudev: Trade, Tariffs, and Empire. Lancashire and British Policy in India, 1919-1939. Delhi 1992.
-Chaudhuri, K.N.: Economic Problems and Indian Independence. In: C.H. Philips and M.D. Wainwright (eds.): The partition of India. Policies and Perspectives 1935-1947. London 1970. S. 310-312.
-Chaudhuri, Pramit: The Indian Economy. Poverty and Development. London 1979.
-Clarke, Peter: Churchill's Economic Ideas. In: Robert Blake/ W. Roger Louis: Churchill. Oxford 1993.
-Collins, Lawy/ Lapierre, Dominique: Um Mitternacht die Freiheit. Reinbek 1978.
-Darwin, John: Britain and Decolonisation. The Retreat from Empire in the Post-War World. London 1988.
-David-Néel, Alexandra: Mein Indien. Die abenteuerlichen Reisen einer ungewöhnlichen und mutigen Frau. München 1993.
-Drummond, I.M.: British Economic Policy and the Empire, 1919-1939. London 1972.
-Drummond, I.M.: The floating pound and the sterling area, 1931-1939. London 1981.
-Edwardes, Michael: The Last Years of British India. London 1963.
-Eldridge, P.J.: The politics of foreign aid in India. London 1969.
-Floud, Roderick/ McCloskey, Donald: The Economic History of Britain since 1700. Vol. 2: 1860 to the 1970s.Cambridge 1981.
-Frankel, F.: India's Political Economy. Princeton 1979.

-Fraser, Antonia: Plain Tales from the Raj. Images of British India in the Twentieth Century. London 1975.
-Gadgil, D.R./ Sovani, N.V.: War and Indian Economic Policy. 1943 (Gokhale Institute of Politics and Economics).
-Gadgil, D.R.: Planning and Economic Policy in India. Poona 1961.
-Gandhi, M.K.: An Autobiography or The Story of My Experiments with Truth. London 1982.
-Gardner, Richard N.: Sterling-Dollar Diplomacy in Current Perspective. The Origins and the Prospect of our International Economic Order. New York 1980.
-Gilbert, Martin: Road to Victory: Winston S. Churchill, 1941-1945. London 1986.
-Glendevon, John: The Viceroy at Bay. Lord Linlithgow in India, 1936-1943. London 1971.
-Gosh, Sumiti Kumar: India and the RAJ: 1919-1947. Glory, shame, bondage. Calcutta 1989.
-Grigg, John (Ed.): Nehru Memorial Lectures, 1966-1991. New Delhi 1992.
-Gurtoo, Dukh Haran Nath: India's Balance of Payments (1920-1960). Delhi 1961.
-Hawtrey, R.G.: Towards the Rescue of Sterling. London 1954.
-Hicks, John: A Theory of Economic History. Oxford 1969.
-India unreconciled: a documented history of Indian political events from the crisis of August 1942 to October 1943. Compiled by Devadas Gandhi. New Delhi 1943.
-India. Council of Scientific and Industrial Research. The wealth of India. 22 Bde., Delhi 1948-1976.
-Indian Federation of Labour. People's plan for economic development of India: being the report of the Post-war Reconstruction Committee of the Indian Federation of Labour. Released by M.N. Roy. Delhi 1944.
-Indian National Congress. National Planning committee, 1938. Report. Ed. by K.T. Shah. Bombay 1949.
-Jathar, G.B./ Beri, S.G.: Elements of Indian economics: being part 2 of Introduction to economics. Madras 1951.
-Jennings, Ivor W./ Ritter, Gerhard A.: Das britische Regierungssystem. Leitfaden und Quellenbuch. Köln und Opladen 1970 (Zweite, überarbeitete und erweiterte Auflage).

-Jha, Prem Shankar: India. A Political Economy of Stagnation. Bombay 1980.
-Joshi, R.M.: Papers and writings on Indian economic and educational problems. Poona 1944.
-Kaushal, G.: Economic history of India, 1757-1966. New Delhi 1979.
-Keynes, J.M.: How to Pay for War. London 1940.
-Keynes, J.M.: Indian Currency and Finance, London 1924.
-Keynes, J.M.: The Economic Consequences of Mr Churchill. London 1925.
-Keynes, J.M.: The General Theory. London 1936.
-Kidron, Michael: Foreign Investments in India. London 1965.
-Konow, Sten: Bedeutung Indiens für England. Hamburg 1932.
-Kulke, Hermann/ Rothermund, Dietmar: Geschichte Indiens. Stuttgart 1982.
-Lakdawala, D.T.: International aspects of Indian economic developments. Bombay 1951.
-Leue, Horst-Joachim: Britische Indienpolitik 1926-1932: Motive, Methoden, Mißerfolge imperialer Politik am Vorabend der Dekolonisation. Wiesbaden 1981.
-Lokanathan, P.S.: India's post-war reconstruction and its international aspects. New Delhi 1946.
-Louis, W. Roger: In the name of god, go! Leo Amery and the British Empire in the age of Churchill. London 1992.
-Lufft, Herrmann: Die Wirtschaft Indiens. Heidelberg 1942.
-Macmillan, Harold: The Middle Way. London 1938.
-Madan, Balkrishna: India and Imperial preference. A study in commercial policy. New Delhi 1939.
-Madgwick, P.J.: Introduction to British Politics. London 1970.
-Mahalanobis, P.C.: The Approach of Operational Research to Planning in India. Calcutta 1955.
-Malenbaum, W.: Modern India's Economy. Two Decades of Planned Growth. Columbus 1971. Bes. Kap. 2: "The Economy at Independence".
-Manchester, William: Winston Churchill. München 1990.
-Markovits, Claude: Indian Business and Nationalist Politics, 1931-1939. The Indigenous Capitalist Class and the Rise of the Congress Party. Cambridge 1985.
-Mesbahuddin, Ahmed: The British Labour Party and The Indian Independent Movement, 1917-1939. New Delhi 1987.

-Middleton, R.: Towards the Managed Economy: Keynes, the Treasury and the Fiscal Policy Debate of the 1930s. London 1985.
-Minhas, B.S.: Planning and the Poor. New Delhi 1974.
-Misra, Babu Ram: Economic aspects of the Indian Constitution. o.O. 1952.
-Moggridge, Donald E.: John Maynard Keynes. München 1977.
-Moore, R.J.: Churchill, Cripps and India. Oxford 1979.
-Moore, R.J.: Endgames of Empire. Studies of Britain's Indian Problem. Delhi 1988.
-Moore, R.J.: Escape from Empire: the Attlee government and the Indian problem. Oxford 1983.
-Morris-Jones, W.H.: The Government and Politics of India. London 1964.
-Mountbatten. Eighty years in pictures. London 1979.
-Mukerjee, Radha Kanand: Economic Problems of Modern India. London 1939.
-Mukkerjee, M.: The National Income of India: Trends and Structure, Calcutta 1969.
-Munshi, K.M.: The ruin that Britain wrought. Bombay 1946.
-Munshi, M.C.: Industrial profits in India, 1936-1944: an inductive study. o.O. 1948.
-Nag, D.S.: A study of economic plans for India. o.O. 1949.
-Narain, Brij: Economic structure of free India. Lahore 1947.
-Narayanaswamy Naidu, B.V.: Indian trade. Annamalainagar 1942.
-Natarajan, L.: American Shadow over India. Bombay 1952.
-Nehru, Jawaharlal: Indiens Weg zur Freiheit. Hamburg 1948.
-Owen, R.H.: India: Economic and Commercial Conditions in India. London 1949.
-Padfield, C.F./ Byrne, A.: British Constitution. London 1972.
-Palekar, S.A.: Commerce. Bombay 1945.
-Pandey, B.N.: South and South-East Asia, 1945-1979. Problems and Politics. London 1979.
-Pandey, Gyanendra (Ed.): The Indian Nation in 1942. Calcutta 1988.
-Parikh, G.D./ M.N. Roy: Alphabet of Fascist Economies - A Critique of the Bombay Plan of Economic Development for India. Calcutta 1944.
-Pilz, H.: Die indische Baumwollindustrie. Berlin 1930.
-Poduval, R.N.: Finance of the Government of India since 1935, Delhi 1951.

-Poduval, R.N.: Recent trends in India's foreign trade. Delhi 1950 (Carty Endowment Lectures 1950).
-Pollard, Sidney: The Development of the British Economy, 1914-1990. London 1992 (Vierte Auflage).
-Postan, M.M.: British War Production. London 1952.
-Prasad, Bishwa Mohan: Second World War and Indian Industry, 1939-45. A Case Study of the Coal Industry in Bengal and Bihar. Delhi 1992.
-Predöhl, Andreas: Das Ende der Weltwirtschaftskrise. Eine Einführung in die Probleme der Weltwirtschaft. Reinbek bei Hamburg 1962.
-Prest, A.R.: The war economies of primary producing countries. Cambridge 1948.
-Ray, R.K.: Industrialisation in India. Growth and Conflict in the Private Corporate Sector, 1914-47. Delhi 1979.
-Reddy, K.N.: The Growth of Public Expenditure in India. New Delhi 1972.
-Rivzi, Gowher: Linlithgow and India. A Study of British Policy and the Political Impasse in India, 1936-1943. London 1978.
-Rosinger, Lawrence Kaelter: India and the United States: political and economic relations. Published under the auspices of the American Institute of Pacific Relations. o.O. 1950.
-Rothermund, Dietmar: An Aspect of the monetary policy of British imperialism. Heidelberg 1970.
-Rothermund, Dietmar: Die politische Willensbildung in Indien, 1900-1960. Wiesbaden 1965 (Schriftenreihe des Südasien-Instituts der Universität Heidelberg).
-Rothermund, Dietmar: India in the Great Depression, 1929-1939. New Delhi 1992.
-Rothermund, Dietmar: Indiens wirtschaftliche Entwicklung. Von der Kolonialherrschaft bis zur Gegenwart. Paderborn 1985.
-Rothermund, Dietmar: Indische Geschichte in Grundzügen. Darmstadt 1989 (Dritte Auflage).
-Rothermund, Dietmar: Mahatma Gandhi. Der Revolutionär der Gewaltlosigkeit. Eine politische Biographie. München 1989.
-Rothermund, Dietmar: Staat und Gesellschaft in Indien. Mannheim 1993.
-Rothermund, Dietmar: The Indian Economy under British Rule and other Essays. New Delhi 1983.
-Royle, Trevor: The last days of the RAJ. London 1989.

-Sardesai, D.R.: British Trade and Expansion in Southeast Asia. Delhi 1977.

-Sarkar, B.K.: Indian Currency and Reserve Bank Problems, 1926-1933. Calcutta 1933.

-Sayers, S.R.: Financial policy, 1939-45. London 1956 (History of the Second World War. United Kingdom Civil Series. Ed. by Sir Keith Hancock).

-Schweinitz' jr, Karl de: The rise and fall of British India. Imperialism as Inequality. London 1983.

-Sen, Sudhir: Deutschland und die indische Wirtschaft. Stuttgart 1937.

-Shah, K.T.: Sixty Years of Indian Finance. Bombay 1937.

-Shriman Narayan: The Gandhian plan of economic development for India. Bombay 1944.

-Singh, R.V.: Essays on economic and commercial problems. Agra 1952.

-Sovani, N.V. (Ed.): Reports of the Commodity Prices Board, Poona 1948.

-Sovani, N.V.: Planning of post-war economic development in India. Published in co-operation with the International Secretariat, Institute of Pacific Relations. 1951 (Gokhale Institute of Politics and economics).

-Sovani, N.V.: The international position of India's raw materials. New Delhi 1948.

-Spear, Percival: A History of India. Vol. II. London 1965.

-Srinivasan, T.N./ Bardhan, P.K. (Ed.): Poverty and Income Distribution in India. Calcutta 1977.

-Stettinius, Edward R.: Lend-Lease. New York 1944.

-Streeten, P./ Lipton, M. (Eds.): The Crisis of Indian Planning. London 1968.

-Sundrum, R.M.: Growth and income distribution in India: policy and performance since independence. New Delhi 1987.

-Suri, Promila/ Zaidi, I.: Impact of British rule on Indian economy. New Delhi 1985.

-Thakurdas, P. et al.: A Brief Memorandum Outlining a Plan of Economic Development for India. Bombay 1944.

-Tidrick, Kathryn: Empire and the English Character. London 1992.

-Tischer, Helmut: Die wirtschaftliche Entwicklung Indiens in den Jahren 1951-1978 unter besonderer Berücksichtigung der Auslandshilfe. Berlin (Ost) 1981.

-Tomlinson, B.R.: The Political Economy of th RAJ, 1914-1947. London 1979.

-Vakil, C.N./ Brahmananda, P.R.: Planning for an Expanding Economy. Bombay 1956.
-Vakil, Chandulal Nagindas: Economic consequences of divided India: a study of the economy of India and Pakistan. o.O. 1950.
-Varshney, R.L.: India's foreign trade during and after the second world war. Allahabad 1954.
-Venkataramani, M.S./ Shrivastava, B.K.: Roosevelt, Gandhi, Churchill. America and the Last Phase of India's Freedom Struggle. New Delhi 1983.
-Venkatasubbiah, H.: Indian Economy since Independence. Bombay 1958.
-Visram, Rozina: Ayahs, Lascars and Princes. The story of Indians in Britain 1700-1947. London 1986.
-Vivesvaraya, M.: A Planned Economy for India. Bangalore 1934.
-Voigt, Johannes H.: Indien im Zweiten Weltkrieg. Stuttgart 1978 (Studien zur Zeitgeschichte. Hrsg. vom Institut für Zeitgeschichte).
-Vyas, Mukund: Männer und Mächte in Indien. Heidelberg 1942.
-Ward Barbara: India and the West. London 1961.
-Watson, Francis: India. A concise history. London 1974.
-Wehler, Hans-Ulrich (Hrsg.): Geschichte und Ökonomie. Königstein/ Ts. 1985.
-Woodcock, George: Who killed the British Empire? London 1974.
-Zinkin, Maurice and Taya: Britain and India: Requiem for Empire. London 1964.
Hancock, W.K./ Gowing, M.M.: British War Economy. London 1949.

Kolibri 360 GmbH
Ferdinand-Jühlke-Straße 7
99095 Erfurt, Deutschland
produktsicherheit@kolibri360.de

Druck:
CPI Druckdienstleistungen GmbH
im Auftrag der
Kolibri 360 GmbH
Ferdinand-Jühlke-Str. 7
99095 Erfurt